DON'T LET YOUR PARTICIPLES DANGLE IN PUBLIC!

A fun, easy-to-understand
guide to American usage
and writing styles.

1990 edition—fully revised and updated
for the new decade.

by M. Kay duPont, CSP
America's #1
Correspondence Trainer

D0366689

Published by Jedco Publishing
2137 Mount Vernon Road
Atlanta, GA 30338
404-395-7483

Introduction

"The study of grammar is dry. It engages not the passions," wrote the crabbed William Cobbett. M. Kay duPont disagrees. She has fun with grammar. You can tell from the title of this book, and you can tell from the subtitle—"A fun, easy-to-understand guide." (Do you object to *fun* as an adjective? The author knows whereof she writes: *fun* has been used adjectivally since 1863.)

In an age of glowing television screens, bleeping video games, and eroding grammar, vocabulary, and Latin study in our schools, we need **DON'T LET YOUR PARTICIPLES DANGLE IN PUBLIC!** For instance, during 1988, Dunkin' Donuts, which boasts of the freshness of its products, ran a radio and TV commercial explaining that "the problem with supermarket doughnuts is there's no telling how long they've been laying there." Disney Pictures and Amblin Entertainment, for another instance, proved the need for this book when they titled one of their films—the fourth most popular of the summer of 1989—*Honey, I Shrunk the Kids.*

By studying M. Kay duPont's words about words, you can avoid laying an egg (albeit a fresh one) and shrinking the language. More important, you will find that grammar, usage, spelling, punctuation, and style are learnable skills. And you'll have fun learning, thanks to the nourishing content, realistic examples, concise format, engaging poems, and sprightly drawings (done by the author herself) that fill this handy handbook.

Richard Lederer
Author of "Anguished English," "Get Thee to a
Punnery," and "Crazy English"
Vice President of SPELL (Society for the Preservation of
English Language and Literature)

ABOUT THE AUTHOR

M. Kay duPont, CSP, is an international consultant in the
field of human communications: Business Writing,
Professional Image, Public Speaking, and Interpersonal
Skills. She is founder and Vice President of **duPont and
Disend Inc.**, an Atlanta company that designs and conducts
communications programs for corporations and associations
all over the world. She's long been known as America's #1
Correspondence Trainer.

Kay had over 15 years
experience as a secre-
tary, office manager, and
legal assistant before
becoming a communica-
tions consultant for the
many corporations,
speakers, and writers
that use her talents. In
addition, she has been a
lecturer at 14 universi-
ties on the proper use of
the English language.

Kay is an award-winning
writer and speaker. She
has won many competi-
tions, including the
Georgia Championship of Public Speaking twice, the
Southeast Region, and fourth place in the World
Championship! She's been awarded the coveted Certified
Speaking Professional designation. . .one of only 200 such
designations in the world. She has also won awards in every
field of writing—from children's literature to news articles.

She is past president of Georgia Speakers Association, and a
member of National Speakers Association, Professional
Secretaries International, International Platform Association,
American Society of Training and Development, and
National Association of Female Executives. She's also
listed in *Who's Who of American Women*.

Other Products By M. Kay duPont

Books

The Great Communicators—A communications anthology

Illusions and Dreams—Poetry for youth

Business Etiquette and Professionalism—A guide to today's business etiquette

Audiocassettes

Communication is More Than Words—A six-cassette program on six different communication topics

The Magic Is YOU!—How to set goals, communicate with your own inner power, believe in yourself, improve your attitude and performance, and be the best you can

The Fine Art of Public Speaking—A comprehensive review of the #1 fear of the American people

How To Communicate Your Ideas—Will help you communicate more clearly and effectively, whether you're in a one-on-one situation or addressing a group

Ten Steps to Better Business Writing—How to make your writing easier, clearer, more concise, and less painful

What is a Professional?—From P to L, Kay covers the main characteristics of successful, professional people in all walks of life

Newsletter

Office Proficiency—a monthly communications newsletter

You might also be interested in Kay's in-house corporate training programs for both management and support staff. If so, call us at 404-395-7483.

Write to publisher for details.
To reorder this book, use form on reverse side.

ORDER FORM

Please send me _____ copies* of **DON'T LET YOUR PARTICIPLES DANGLE IN PUBLIC!**
I'm enclosing:

$14.95 x number of books	$_____
Georgia residents add 5% sales tax	$_____
Postage and handling, first book	$____2.50_____
$1.00 postage for each additional book	$_____
TOTAL	$_____

*5% discount for five for more

NAME:_____

TITLE:_____

COMPANY:_____

ADDRESS:_____

CITY, STATE, ZIP:_____

AREA CODE, PHONE:_____

    Please also send me information about your programs for companies and associations for the
_____management   _____midmanagement
_____staff level

Mail forms to: Jedco Publishing
2137 Mt. Vernon Road
Atlanta, GA 30338
404-395-7483

TABLE OF CONTENTS

Chapter 4: Sentence Structure

Chapter 5: Style of Writing

Chapter 6: Spelling

Chapter 10: Letters

**Good writers are not born;
they are created by their own hands.**

CHAPTER 1: FOREWORD

Why did I write this book?

For four reasons:

(1) To try to give others some of my love of, and fascination with, words and the English language.

(2) To provide a light, easy-to-read, informative usage guide that you can keep at your desk, or by your favorite chair, or in your pocket (if you have a large pocket). I only hope you don't put it on a shelf in a bookcase with your copy of the 1968 phone directory.

(3) To answer many of the questions I hear in my training classes. The questions are usually the same from person to person, company to company, year to year.

(4) To bring you up to date with grammar and style changes.

Let me first answer some of the more general questions:

Why do we need to learn to communicate better? Isn't what we mean more important than what we say?

There's a very definite answer to that last part: Yes. . .and no. I'm not really being ambiguous. Of course it's important to say what you mean, but communication should be more than just getting your point across. You should make a conscious effort to convey your ideas

I might as well be talking to Quarqfark, the six-headed borensterk from the planet of Zamoo.

in the best, most precise, most understandable manner. I may be the greatest wordsmith in the world, but if you don't fully understand what I mean, we're not communicating effectively. I might as well be talking to Quarqfarq, the six-headed borensterk from the planet of Zamoo.

I believe our language is the most important part of our lives. It's what sets us apart from the animals—and from each other. Our words are the cornerstones of everything we feel, believe, and obtain; they have an impact on every aspect of our lives. Our language is the backbone of our economy and free enterprise system, because it's through language that companies buy, sell, and render services. It's through our words that we express our innermost thoughts and acknowledge the feelings of others. It's through our language that our schools, governments, judicial systems, and every other aspect of our lives are run.

Whether you're an office supervisor, a plant manager, a secretary, a homemaker, or a hockey-puck polisher, you're faced daily with word choices. But because our language is complex, and often confusing, many people never bother to learn the correct way to use it.

1.2

That's too bad. I have discovered a painful maxim in my studies: *If it's possible to be misunderstood, you will be*. My experience has shown that too many people live by the motto: *I know you believe you understand what you think I said, but I'm not sure you realize that what you heard is not what I meant.*

Have you ever had a disagreement with your manager or secretary or coworkers because what you wrote down was not interpreted correctly? Have you ever had an argument with your spouse or in-laws or children because what you meant was not what they heard you say? Can you truth-fully say that you've never had a communications misunderstanding?

If you always choose your words correctly, never have any trouble with spelling, and punctuate like a wizard, congrat-ulations! You're just reading this book because you don't have anything better to do, and I thank you!

I have a feeling, however, that you're reading this book because now and then you have a problem with your com-munication, or find yourself in doubt about how to say or write something. If your pen has ever faltered, your hand ever fumbled at your typewriter, or your tongue ever stuck to your teeth as you probed your brain for the right word or sentence structure, read on!

Are grammar and usage more important than vocabulary?

Vocabulary is certainly important, but I believe the skill to weave words together and use them to their best advantage is even more vital. The magic wand required for this ability is grammar.

Magic wand? Sure! There's no magic in words, only in the disciplined use of them. Is there magic in a rabbit? Not usually. A rabbit will sit in a concealed box all day; it takes a skilled hand to bring it from that box through a top hat and onto a stage. It's still a rabbit, but now, with the right magic wand, it's a very special rabbit.

With the right magic wand, even rabbits can be special.

So it is with communication. Words—as irreplaceable as they are—are only words; it takes a careful hand and a knowledge of the rules to make them most effective.

Why is learning grammar so difficult?

The more I work with businesses and individuals to help them communicate more effectively, the more I realize that the major problem with English is its rules, and the major problem with the rules is their complexity.

I believe the study of communication skills and—believe it or not!—grammar <u>can</u> be fun. I know the idea of reading a language guidebook for enjoyment has never occurred to most people, and I can understand why. Somehow the word "grammar" conjures up images of Miss Boring's high-school class and hours spent diagramming sentences and learning dull rules. I can't imagine why grammar is taught that way. To me, the rules are not nearly as important as the logic. I think the study of English—and the proper use of it—should be, and <u>can</u> be, as much fun as studying the strategy of Rubik's Cube or Space Invaders.

Grammar has all the qualities of a game. Think of it as putting together a jigsaw puzzle. The pieces of the game are the parts of speech and we have to put them together into a complete picture. Or sometimes we can play like detectives, discovering the relationships between words and phrases. Or lawyers, defending the logic of using a specific clause or structuring a sentence the way we think best.

Sometimes we play like detectives, discovering the relationships between words and phrases and clauses.

So what grammar really requires is the ability to analyze, make judgments, and act on our decisions. If you can follow the instructions for a dress pattern, trace the wiring in a house, put in spark plugs, read a cookbook, or keep up with the day-to-day problems of running a home or an office, understanding grammar should be no problem at all.

Are there different levels of usage?

Sure, and none of us stays on the same level all the time. We move easily back and forth from the basement of slang and substandard usage (with our friends at the bowling alley) to the family room of everyday usage (with our business cohorts) to the penthouse of formal usage (with a prospective employer or creditor). But we must be constantly aware of where we are and our level of usage so we don't fall below what's expected of us at that particular time and place.

Loues Laboursloft.

A WITTIE AND
PLEASANT
COMEDIE,

As it was Acted by his Maiefties Seruants at
the Blacke-Friers *and the* Globe,

Written

By **WILLIAM SHAKESPEARE.**

LONDON,

Printed by *W.S.* for *Iohn Smethwicke,* and are to be
fold at his Shop in Saint *Dunftones* Church-
yard vnder the Diall.

What we're going to discuss in this book are some of the problems we face in the family room of standard, informal English. **Standard English** is that of educated, careful users of the language (and that includes <u>most</u> of us <u>most</u> of the time). **Informal English** is <u>correct</u> usage, suitable in all everyday speaking <u>and</u> writing. We'll leave slang and formality for another book.

Do the rules change?

Yes, indeed. English, like most languages, is a living entity and changes regularly. That's one of the things that has always fascinated me. It's changed so much that dear Mr. Shakespeare wouldn't be able to even <u>read</u> this book, much less understand it. I have a book of poetry by Robert Burns that I can't read because it hasn't been translated from <u>his</u> English into <u>ours</u>.

"Sure," you say, "but that was a long time ago. Things were different then. People talked funny, and their spelling, why, it was absurd!" Was it? Is *amang* any stranger than *among*? Is the reasoning behind *before* or *between* any more logical than the reasoning behind *afore* or *atween*? Does *barefooted* make more sense than *barefit* or *barefeeted*? Not to me, but my opinion is not the issue here.

Somewhere between Robert Burns' time and ours, *awnie* became *bearded* and *auldfarran* became *sagacious* and we lost the diminutive form altogether. (I rather like *beastie* and *ghostie* and *bardie*. We have no such degrees of size or awesomeness anymore, and *beastie* says so much more than *little beast*.)

So, yes, the rules have changed. They have changed in your lifetime; they have changed this year. People who write dictionaries can be only historians, because all they can do is record how words have been used in the *past*. By the time a dictionary gets to the bookstore, some word has

> Hawaet we Gar-Dean in geardagum theodcynginga thrym gefrunon
> hu that aethelingas ellen fremedon.
>
> Listen! We have learned of the glory of the kings of the
> Spear-Danes in days of yore, how the princes did deeds of valor.
> --Beowulf

been added to, or deleted from, our language simply because the people began or stopped using it. Remember when there were no such words as *palimony, watergate, timewise*? when *judgment* had an "e" in it? when *real estate* was hyphenated? when *Edsel* was a car (and, before that, a person), and not a definition of something (or someone) that has failed? when *gay* and *aids* were words we could use in public?

Some expressions, once considered slang or colloquial, are now used regularly by both speakers and writers (*OK*); nouns are used as adjectives and verbs (*impactfully, concretize*); adjectives are used as prepositions (*absent*); proper names have become verbs (*to Xerox*); and absolutes are being compared (*emptier*). New words have been born (*legalese*), old words have died (*whence, amongst*), and we use words in our everyday communications that would have made my granddaddy's two strands of white hair curl!

It's all right now to begin a sentence with a conjunction like *and* or *but*, end it with a preposition (except *at*), and split your infinitives.

So you see, communication today has been liberated from many of its chains. It's more flexible. It has become a stretch language; one size fits all. It's a language in which we use opposites interchangeably (*ravel/unravel; flammable/inflammable; fat chance/slim chance/no chance*), and in which we use synonyms as antonyms (*odor/aroma*).

We can—and should—enjoy the flexibility, but we can't go crazy and lose all sense of discipline, because many of the rules and guidelines are steadfast and not open to personal preference or what feels right.

1.7

If you use punctuation improperly, or use substandard words like *irregardless, enthused, authored, ain't,* or *couth*; or fail to recognize the difference between homonyms like *affect* and *effect,* you could destroy the respect and confidence you want to build in your employers, colleagues, customers, and friends. When you're groping for the best way to put your thoughts into words, knowing the rules will make it a lot easier for you and, as a result, your communication will be more effective.

A mastery of usage requires reading, listening, and checking whenever you're unsure. Buy a new dictionary every five years and keep <u>this</u> book close by. It's to be used as both a reference book <u>and</u> a study guide. It's an easy, enjoyable, conversational "roadmap" to help you become more familiar with the words you use.

We're going to discuss what's proper and improper in today's normal usage. I'm going to share some of the simple memory tricks (*mnemonics,* for you purists and trivia buffs) and easy guidelines I've learned over the years that will help you avoid the pitfalls and improve your day-to-day communications. I chose the material I thought would be most beneficial to most people. I believe most of you know that sentences begin with a capital letter and end with a period, and I doubt that you are overly concerned with the definition of a gerund or the future perfect tense. I just want to simplify the most important usages so you can use them more easily.

If you use our language correctly often enough, it will become a habit, just as poor usage will. Language is like love—it's there for you to enjoy if you'll just see the beauty.

If you're so smart, Kay, why aren't you rich?

If I were that smart, my friends, I would not only be rich—I'd be beautiful as well.

1.8

My knowledge and information come from many sources. The writing/publishing/speaking/teaching world is filled with "experts" on the English language. I've included a bibliography at the end of the book so you can continue your study if you wish. The study of language is as old as people themselves. The printing press remains one of the greatest inventions of all times because, through the printed word, we have access to all the years of study and hard work that others have completed. I don't care to ever reinvent the wheel, although I am pleased with my invention of the punctuation light (Chapter 9) and my simplification of compound pronouns (Chapter 8).

Precisely because English is a living language and the rules are constantly changing, however, the experts often differ. I've tried to give you a consensus of the experts I believe in and an accumulation of my studies, with a measure of common sense and a dash of personal preference thrown in.

For those few areas of disagreement, I've sided with *Webster's New World Dictionary, Third College Edition* and *Webster's Guide to Business Correspondence.*

Although there are some matters others will disagree on, all of us are steadfast on certain rules. I'll try to let you know as we go along which are which. If, however, you find any blatant errors, please let me know so I can correct them. Somehow it doesn't seem right for an English guidebook to contain errors. (And thanks to all of you who have contributed suggestions for past editions!)

You may not realize when your participles are dangling in public. . .but others will!

CHAPTER 2: GLOSSARY

Absolute: A modifier that can't change degrees of intensity because it is already total. For example: *perfect, unique, equal, final, first, last, fatal, total, unanimous, surrounded, pregnant, dead.*

Acronym: A word formed from the first (or first few) letters of a series of words. ***Radio detecting and ranging=radar***

Active Voice: The verb form used when the subject performs the action, when the format of the sentence is Subject, Verb, Object: *I hit the ceiling.*

Adjective: Modifies a noun or pronoun. May be a single word, a phrase, or a clause.

> **Attributive** adjectives precede the nouns they modify: ***small** child.*

> **Demonstrative** adjectives are used to point out something: ***That** book.*

> **Descriptive** adjectives name the quality or condition of the word they modify: ***dull** pencil.*

Interrogative adjectives as a question: *Whose coat is that?*

Predicate adjectives come after the verb *to be* or some other linking verb: *The soup was **cold**.*

Adverb: Modifies a verb, adjective, or another adverb. May be a single word, a phrase, or a clause.

Appositive: A word, phrase, or clause placed near a noun to explain it and having the same grammatical relation to the rest of the sentence as the word it describes. It's fluff. Always set off by commas: *My boss,* the attorney, *sends me flowers every Secretaries Day.*

Article: The words *a, an, the. A* and *an* normally refer to nonspecific items—*an* apple can be any apple. *The* normally refers to specific items—*the* apple must be the only apple in question.

Case: The way the relationship of a noun or pronoun to the rest of the sentence is shown. There are three cases: Nominative (subject), Objective (object), and Possessive (ownership).

Clause: A group of words that contains at least one subject and it's verb.

Independent (coordinate) clauses have the same rank and are connected by a comma and a coordinating conjunction: *It started to snow, so we left the party.*

Dependent (subordinate) clauses are dependent on another clause and can't stand alone. They answer the questions *when, where, why,* or *how. She always eats a bowl of ice cream before she goes to bed.*

Nonrestrictive clauses are parenthetical and could be omitted without changing the meaning. They are surrounded by commas: *My cat, which is pink and green, purrs a lot.*

Cliche: Comes from the French *clicher*, meaning "to stereotype," which means "to make a printing plate from a matrix or mold from set type." The idea is of a hard and fixed thing. Other qualities are triteness and boredom. For example: *Too funny for words, sweet as sugar.*

Colloquialism: Informal quality, style, or usage: *Ain't, you know, gonna, gotta.*

Comparative: Modifiers that change degrees of intensity, up or down: *small, smaller, smallest.*

Complex Sentence: A sentence consisting of one independent clause and one or more dependent (subordinate) clauses.

Compound: Consisting of two or more elements.

A **compound noun** consists of two words that may have been used separately at one time but now are combined, often with a hyphen.

A **compound sentence** consists of two or more independent clauses.

A **compound subject** consists of two or more subjects having the same verb.

A **compound verb** consists of two or more verbs having the same subject.

Compound-complex sentence: A sentence that contains more than one independent clause and at least one subordinate clause.

Conjunction: A word or group of words that connects other words or groups of words: *and, but, for*.

Conjunctive Adverb: An adverb that connects two sentences. It shows a relationship between the sentences and is preceded by a semicolon and followed by a comma: *However, instead, therefore, furthermore, besides, indeed*.

Contraction: The shortening of a word or phrase by the omission of one or more sounds or letters: *she's* for *she is*.

Dangling Participle: A modifier that is positioned in the wrong place in the sentence (usually dangling at the end) to properly modify what it's supposed to.

Declarative sentence: A sentence that makes a statement.

Euphemism: An expression used to avoid a disagreeable subject: *pass away* instead of *die.*

Expletive: An oath or exclamation, especially an obscenity.

Footnote: A note of comment or reference at the bottom of a page.

Fluff: A Kayism for unnecessary words, sentences, or paragraphs. Word fluff is usually the when, where, why, and how of the sentence.

Gerund: The *ing* form of a verb that serves as a noun: *I cringe at his singing in the shower.* (Note that gerunds always require a possessive modifier.)

Homograph: A word spelled like another, but of different meaning or origin (*low*=sound made by cattle; *low*=not high or tall). Becomes a problem with words beginning with some prefixes, so homographs continue to carry hyphens after the prefix: *re-cover, re-sign, re-creation, co-op*.

Homonym: A word with the same pronunciation as another but with a different meaning, origin and, usually, spelling: *chord/cord*.

Hyperbole: An expression used to exaggerate: *I could eat a horse*.

Idiomatic Expression: A phrase or expression whose common meaning is different from its literal translation: *That story **sounds fishy** to me*.

Imperative sentence: A sentence that gives a mild command or request.

Infinitive: The form of a verb used with *to*. Split infinitives (insertion of a word between *to* and the verb) are now acceptable.

Interjection: An exclamation inserted into an utterance without grammatical connection to it: *Aha!*

Intransitive Verb: A verb that does not require an object to complete its meaning.

Jargon: Strange, confused, or obscure language that is not intelligible **or,** more commonly, language of a particular specific group.

Leader: The horizontal guiding line (usually a row of periods) between a chapter title and the page number it starts on.

Misplaced Modifier: A modifier that gives an unclear reference because it's incorrectly placed in a sentence. Often a dangling participle.

Modifier: A word (adjective or adverb) or phrase that describes another word or phrase.

Nonrestrictive Elements: Words, phrases, or clauses that are not essential to the meaning of the sentence. Fluff.

Noun: A word that names a person, place, thing, quality, or act.

Object: A word or group of words that receives, or is affected by, the action of a verb. The "doee" that is acted on.

Parallel structure: Similar wording or arrangement of words in a sentence or series of sentences: *I came, I saw, I conquered.*

Participle: A word formed from a verb that is used as an adjective. It ends in *ing*: **Going** *to the store, I saw some of my friends.*

Passive Voice: The verb form used when the subject is the receiver of the action, when the format of the sentence is Object, Verb, Subject: *The ceiling was hit.*

Person: Denotes the speaker (first person), the person spoken to (second person), or the person or thing spoken about (third person).

Personification: Attributing human characteristics to non-human subjects.

Phrase: A group of words, without a subject and its verb, that function as a single part of speech.

Plural: More than one of something.

Possessive Case: Shows ownership of nouns and pronouns.

Predicate: The part of a sentence that tells what the subject does, did, or will do.

Prefix: A word element attached to the front of a base word that changes the meaning of the base word. Usually not hyphenated unless the new word is a homograph.

Preposition: A word that shows the relation between a noun or pronoun and another word in the sentence: *into, through, at.*

Pronoun: Takes the place of a noun in a sentence.

Restrictive Elements: Words, phrases, or clauses essential to the meaning of the sentence.

Run-On Sentence: Two independent clauses written as a single sentence, often joined with only a comma. Also applies to sentences with proper punctuation that ramble on and on.

Sentence Fragment: A group of words that does not contain a complete, stand-alone thought. Usually a clause with no subject or no verb: *Hoping to see you.* OR *As he watched television, turning occasionally to speak to his child.*

Simple Sentence: A sentence with one subject and one predicate.

Slang: Highly informal speech that is outside conventional or standard usage. It consists both of coined words and phrases and of new or extended meanings attached to established terms. Slang develops from the attempt to find colorful, pungent, or humorous expressions, and generally passes into disuse. Slang is seldom acceptable in business writing.

Subject: The part of a sentence about which something is being said. The "doer" that does the action.

Suffix: A word element added to the end of a base word that changes the meaning of the base word. Rarely hyphenated.

Transitive Verb: A verb that requires a direct object to complete its meaning.

Verb: A word that expresses action, being, or occurrence.

Voice: Verb forms used to show action (active or passive).

CHAPTER 3: PARTS OF SPEECH

Why should we review the parts of speech?

Because the eight parts of speech make up every thought we think, every sentence we write, every letter we mail. Punctuation is basically governed by the parts of speech; plurality is governed by the parts of speech; homonyms are easier to decide on if we're familiar with the parts of speech.

So, like building a house, the study of grammar must begin at the bottom. We have to lay the groundwork before we can put up the bricks, build the walls, or paint the moldings. Unfortunately, most adults can only remember the names of some of the parts of speech, and have trouble identifying them in sentences. It's really much easier to write effectively if you have a working knowledge of these eight components.

Okay, what are they?

Noun: From Latin *nomen* (name). Names a person, place, thing, act, or quality: *Kay, Atlanta, chair,* [the] *writing, goodness.* Nouns are essential to our language; they are the heads of our sentence skeletons. Nouns are divided into four classifications: *common* (boy), *proper* (Jan), *abstract* (beauty), and *collective* (group).

Pronoun: From Latin *pro* (before) and *nomen* (verb). Substitutes for a noun: *she, he, it, we, who, whom.* Pronouns are like stunt people in the movies—they fill in for the star (noun) when he or she needs a break. There are three classes of pronouns: subjective, objective, and possessive (**See Chapter 8**).

Adverb: From Latin *ad* (to, toward) and *verbum* (verb). Modifies, limits, or describes a verb, adjective, or another adverb: *happily, very.* Often answers the question "how."

Adjective: From Latin *adjectivum* (something added). Modifies, limits, or describes a noun or pronoun: *beautiful, ugly.* Adjectives often answer the questions: what kind, which one, how many, how much, where, when, why, or how.

There are three common types of adjectives.

> **Descriptive** adjectives name the quality or condition of the word they modify. When a descriptive adjective precedes the noun it modifies, it's called **attributive:** *small* child, *pretty* flower, *accurate* survey. When the descriptive adjective comes after some form of the verb *to be* or some other linking verb, it's called a **predicate adjective:** *The day was* hot. *The sky is* cloudless. *I want to be* alone.
>
> **Interrogative** adjectives ask a question: *Whose* book is this?
>
> **Demonstrative** adjectives are used to point out something: *This* child, *that* office.

Verb: From Latin *verbum* (word). Expresses action or state of being: *go, is.* Verbs tell us either what our subject *is* or what it's *doing.*

Conjunction: From Latin *conjungere* (to join). Conjunctions are like railroad depots—they connect words or phrases so they won't run over each other: *and, but, for.*

Interjection: From Latin *inter* (among, between, into) and *jectum* (thrown). Interjections modify nothing, show no action, and have no job in a sentence except to express strong feeling or excitement. An interjection often stands alone, and is usually followed by an exclamation mark: *Aha!* It can simply be separated from the rest of the sentence by commas: *Well, you see, I found you!*

Preposition: From Latin *prae* (before) and *positum* (placed). Shows relationship between a noun or pronoun and another word. Prepositions are the detectives of grammar—they tell us what, when, where, or how: *into the room, at the movies, through the door.* "Where" is its most common reference.

What about the old rule about not using prepositions at the end of a sentence? To paraphrase Winston Churchill, that rule is nonsense up with which we should not put. The structure was originally formulated in the 17th century by the English poet, John Dryden, who based his reasoning on the structure of Latin. Luckily, this rule has been almost dropped from the rulebook.

Sometimes placing the preposition at the end does make a weak sentence, and *at* is still not considered good usage at the end of a sentence. But an idiomatic sentence such as *"They don't know what they're talking about"* puts the

PARTS OF SPEECH

A **NOUN** is a person, place, act, quality, or thing,
Or sometimes even a time, like *today* or *spring*;
A **NOUN** is the name of anything,
Like *kindness, garden, love,* or *swing.*

Instead of nouns, the **PRONOUNS** stand;
Her toes, *his* face, *our* arms, *your* hand;
A **PRONOUN** takes the noun's true place,
Like *they* for people, *she* for Grace.

VERBS tell what the subject does,
Like *loves* or *hates*, *is* or *was*;
VERBS tell of acts being done:
Read, dance, laugh, type, run.

An **ADJECTIVE** describes a noun,
Like *gay* or *ugly*, *rich* or *brown*;
An **ADJECTIVE** modifies a pronoun,
Like *great, small, up, down.*

ADVERBS tell us where or when,
Like *up, down, now, then*;
How things are done **ADVERBS** also tell,
Like *nicely, fast, bad, well.*

A **PREPOSITION** stands before a noun:
In bed, *at* sea, *to* town;
So the **PREPOSITION** comes before,
Like *through* or *around* the open door.

CONJUNCTIONS join words together,
Like cats *or* dogs, fowl *and* feather;
CONJUNCTIONS are a bridge across:
But, like, as, because.

An **INTERJECTION**, last of all,
Like *oh!* and *ouch!*, is very small;
An **INTERJECTION** shows surprise,
Like *Who me?, How nice!, Bless my eyes!*

stress where it belongs—at the end. *"They don't know about what they're talking"* sounds silly. In fact, some-times a preposition at the end of a sentence is required to avoid improper construction, as in *"The plan was agreed to"* or *"The clothes haven't been gone through."* The end preposition is common in passive-verb constructions like those, and also in many idiomatic expressions like *"I'm fed up"* or *"You turn me on."*

And a preposition often fits best at the end of a question. If you try to avoid it, you'll probably end up with a stilted question. *"What are you thinking about?"* is much better than *"About what are you thinking?"* and *"What did you do that for?"* is better than *"For what did you do that?"*

CHAPTER 4:
SENTENCE STRUCTURE

What is a sentence?

A sentence is a group of words that has a beginning and an ending and makes sense all by itself. The beginning is called the **subject** (usually a noun or pronoun), and the ending is called the **predicate**. The subject is the person, place, or thing in the sentence; the predicate tells us something about the subject.

A subject can be as simple as "*Cats,*" or as complicated as "*Long-tailed, yellow-and-brown, lovely (but temperamental) Calico cats. . . .*" A predicate can be as simple as ". . .*purr,*" or as complicated as ". . .*purr loudly when they feel like being friendly and showing you how much they love you, and sometimes even when they are angry.*" Even in the second examples, the subject is still "*Cats*" and the primary predicate is still "*purr.*" Whether short or long, the thought is complete and can stand alone. No matter how complicated we make our cats or their purring, the skeleton is still *"Cats purr."* Everything else is fluff.

In English, there are four types of sentences: **simple, compound, complex,** and **compound-complex.** It's probably not too important for you, as a professional, to be able to diagram a sentence or know a great deal about complex and compound-complex sentences. But if you want to write correctly, you <u>must</u> <u>know</u> what a simple sentence is, and it will sure help if you can recognize a compound sentence.

Simple

A simple sentence is one subject (who/what), one verb (do/does/did what), one complement (to whom/what)—in that order. Again, think of your sentence as a skeleton:

WHO	*DO WHAT*	*TO WHOM*	*WHEN*
Cats	*eat*	*mice*	*when hungry.*

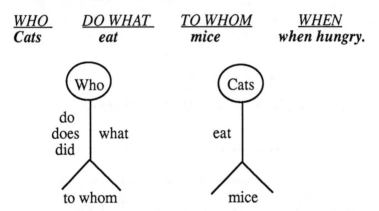

Individual modifiers shouldn't change your structure either:

WHO	*DO WHAT*	*TO WHOM*
Fat cats	*ravenously eat*	*frightened mice*

WHEN
when very hungry.

Your skeleton still has a head (*cats*), a body (*eat*), and feet (*mice*).

Sometimes, of course, you really won't have feet; and that's OK:

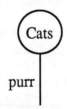

4.2

The thought can still stand alone, even without feet! It's still a **simple sentence**—one subject, one predicate, one complete thought.

Sometimes you'll add other parts to your skeleton, but they're always fluff—complements—never structure, so they belong at the end: Who Did What To Whom. . .When Where Why How.

Compound

If we were to add a conjunction, a comma, and another complete thought, the sentence would become compound:

Cats purr happily, but I prefer dogs.

A **compound sentence** has two complete thoughts, each with a subject <u>and</u> a predicate, each independent of the other. A compound sentence is just two simple sentences joined by a conjunction <u>and</u> a comma.

Complex

A **complex sentence** consists of one independent clause (skeleton) and one or more dependent (subordinate) clauses (fluff):

>*Customers may make monthly payments if they wish.*

Compound-complex

A **compound-complex** sentence contains two or more independent clauses and one or more dependent clauses:

>*Customers may make monthly payments if they wish, but customers who don't pay cash will be charged interest on the unpaid balance.*

Recognizing these elements will help you write all your sentences, no matter how complicated. It doesn't matter how long or complex a sentence becomes, every subject must have a predicate (can be just a verb) and every predicate must have a subject. If that's not true, you probably have either a sentence fragment or a run-on sentence.

Fragment

A **sentence fragment** is a group of words that doesn't contain both a subject <u>and</u> a predicate, such as this excerpt from the menu of a prominent restaurant:

>*You can dine and see the beautiful view. As unique as the restaurant itself.*

The first group of words is a subject *(you)* with a compound verb *(can dine and see).* The last group of words is only a phrase. It doesn't have a subject (who) <u>or</u> a verb (do what), and it doesn't make sense by itself.

The next examples illustrate the confusion fragments can cause:

> *We prepared the statistics, and they prepared the report.* **Sending by separate mail.** (who is?)

> *In the spring when the weather is warmer, many of us feel a bit restless.* **Wishing to take a day off from work.** (who is?)

Even though sentence fragments don't make sense, many people use them regularly. Try not to. They work all right in advertising, for emphasis, but should be avoided in business writing.

WHO IS SENDING WHAT TO WHOM?

Run-on

Equally in error is a **run-on sentence**—one that contains
<u>too</u> <u>many</u> subjects or predicates. A run-on sentence is
created by joining two complete thoughts with only a
comma instead of a comma-conjunction combination or a
semicolon:

> *I like this book about marshmallows, I'm soft on
> them.*

> *We received the letter yesterday, it arrived in the
> mail.*

> *The speaker had stage fright, he shook all over.*

Each of these examples should be written as two sentences,
or combined with a semicolon, since each component
expresses a separate, complete, thought. Of course you
could also add an appropriate conjunction and keep the
comma.

There are only three ways to combine complete declarative
thoughts: a comma/conjunction combination, a semicolon,
or a period. Nothing else will convey the meaning you
want.

These ideas become vitally important when you're trying to
decide whether to use a singular or plural verb in a sentence, what kind of punctuation is correct, and whether
your reader will understand what you mean.

How long should a sentence be?

That depends on what you want to say. Sometimes it takes longer to express one idea than it does another.

The most effective writing, however, is concise. As we have already seen, *"Cats purr"* is a perfectly understandable sentence. But not all your sentences will be—or should be—that elementary. Still, a sentence should contain no unnecessary words, and a paragraph no unnecessary sentences, for the same reasons that a drawing should have no extra lines and a machine no extra parts.

Simple sentences make all communication—speeches, reports, letters—more understandable. The emphasis of a sentence should lie not in its length, but in its words. The longer your sentences, the longer your letter, the less likely it is to be read. It's not easy to write simply; it's much easier to be complex or to ramble. But once you get the hang of it, it's a lot more fun, a lot quicker, and a lot less energy-consuming to write the way you speak.

This doesn't mean we have to make all our sentences short, although short sentences <u>are</u> more easily understood by the average reader. It also doesn't mean we have to avoid all detail and always treat our subjects simply. It just means we should write the way we speak, and we seldom use long sentences in our speech. Overly long sentences tend to drag readers into complacency. They also demand a good memory, because the readers have to hold on to the statement in the first phrase until they wade through all the commas and fluff and reach the connecting point in the final phrase.

For a guideline, try Kay's Rule of Max: Keep your maximum length to one page per letter, ten paragraphs per page, ten sentences per paragraph, twenty words per sentence, three syllables per word.

Kay's Rule of Max

1 page per letter
10 paragraphs per page
10 sentences per paragraph
20 words per sentence
3 syllables per word

CHAPTER 5:
STYLE OF WRITING

What is style?

Style in business correspondence, like language, has changed to meet the demands of its users. In fact, it changes regularly.

However, there's one basic principle that can't be repeated often enough and will never change again: **Write the way you speak** (within professional limits, of course)! Imagine the reader sitting in front of you—what would you <u>say</u>?

The trouble with many letter writers is that they don't express their true personalities in their correspondence. They write as if they were ancient creatures with petrified voice boxes and fossilized brains. They pretend a business letter is a formal document, and use stale phrases like *enclosed herewith you will please find, thank you in advance, we beg to advise you.*

Why? Why should contacting people by mail be any different from contacting them in person or on the phone? They are the same people, with the same feelings and emotions. If anything, you should try even harder to be friendly because you're working under a handicap—you're not there to correct any wrong impressions your words might make.

Suppose I came up to you and said, "*I am pleased to hand you herewith your check payable in the amount of Two Dollars and no cents parenthesis Two Dollars end parenthesis."*

You'd say, *"Huh? What in the world are you talking about?"* or maybe, *"About what in the world are you talking?"*

The most effective style is a <u>natural</u> one. A stiff, formal letter is old-fashioned and has no place in a modern business organization. A letter that's pompous and puts on airs will cause the reader to take it less than seriously. This doesn't mean you have to be silly, of course. It just means that, no matter what your letter's purpose, a friendly, conversational tone will make it more effective, clearer, simpler, briefer, and more likely to succeed.

How do you develop style? Practice. Writing is an art form, just like painting and sculpting. Only you can develop your "style." Read your letter out loud when you're finished—that's the only way you'll know for sure if it sounds natural. If it doesn't, start over.

I am pleased to hand you herewith a reduplication of the matutinal newsworthy, at least informationwise, script of alleged events occurring within our own vicinity, and perchance even within our own viewing area, for your personal matriculation process. . . you know?

When you're analyzing a letter or memo that didn't come out exactly the way you wanted it to, ask yourself, *What was I trying to accomplish?* Think it over until you can state the purpose of the letter in one simple sentence.

When you have the purpose clearly in mind, take another look and ask yourself a few more questions:

- Did I state my purpose straightforwardly and directly, or did I beat around the bush?

- Did I ramble or put in extraneous material?

- Is the letter geared toward my reader?

- Did I talk normally and conversationally?

- Did I anticipate the reader's questions and answer them as I wrote?

- Did I translate all technical terms the reader might have trouble understanding?

- Do my sentences strike the eye and ear as complete, logical units?

- Are my ideas divided into separate paragraphs?

If you can answer *yes* to these questions, you probably have an excellent business letter.

What's the biggest problem with style?

Worditis—that prevalent disease that causes us to ramble. It appears in written <u>and</u> spoken material. It's sometimes called smoke-screening—using confusing words, or too many words,when you really don't want to be understood or you just want to hedge. It often happens when we want to impress people. But if we use words or phrases that sound superior and snobbish to our readers, they won't be impressed, they'll only be confused. Just as it would be ridiculous to use a gun to kill a fly, it's also ridiculous to use pompous words to express modest meaning.

Effective writing is concise, and redundancy is one of the most common time-wasters and message-bloaters in today's business letters. Words are a lot like extra pounds—the more you have, the worse the whole package looks.

Have you ever said, *I myself think. . .* or *I personally believe. . .?* Why? If it's *I*, it <u>has</u> to be *myself* and *personal*.

I often hear phrases like, *I remember that day in my mind.* Where else would you remember? *Put a smile on your face.* Where else would I put one? Then there's the child who's *larger in size* than his sister. In what other way would he be larger?

Some writers will refer to two items being *identically the same.* If they are identical, they <u>are</u> the same. We say that something *follows thereafter*, though how it could follow anywhere else, I don't know. And items are *enclosed herein*, even though enclosed means herein.

And have you noticed how many banks offer *free gifts* for depositing? I've never asked anyone I know to pay for a gift, have you? I've never had anything but tuna *fish*, either.

References to time also cause redundancy. *Early summer* often becomes *the early part of summer*, *7 AM* is referred to as *7:00 AM in the morning*, and *now* becomes *at this present time* or *at this point in time* or *at this current and present point in time.*

If I said that *my cranial habiliment came asunder in a squall,* would you know that my hat blew off in a gust of wind? If I told you that *I had ovum for my matutinal refection,* would you know that I had eggs for breakfast? If I said that *my horological mechanism failed to be efficacious*, would you know that my clock didn't keep time? What if I asked you for a *quadrilabial osculation?*

Using words like those can put our readers in the same bind as Albert Einstein's wife. She was once asked whether she understood everything her famous husband said. "I understand some of the words," she said, "but none of the sentences."

5.4

It isn't hard to write a message that, if someone takes the time to study it, is absolutely clear. But a message that has to be studied isn't a good message. We must choose our words so that our reader will be sure to understand them without waste of time and thought. The meaning of a good letter is so immediately clear and obvious that it doesn't have to be dissected. Word litter is to writing what an amplifier is to chamber music—it ruins the quality.

**QUADRILABIAL
OSCULATION**

How can we avoid worditis?

Think and plan. Economizing with words is just a matter of packing the same, or more, meaning into a smaller unit to save your reader's time and better your chances of communicating what you have to say. It isn't always easy. The idea is so clear to you—you know what you mean—that you may not realize how difficult or confusing your letter will be to someone else. The question to ask yourself is not "Does this word sound important?" but "Is this word necessary?" Not "Did I use enough words to explain it?" but "Did I explain it too much?"

If, of course, some lovely, dramatic, or inspired phrases or sentences come to you while you're writing, fine. Put them in. But then, with cold, objective eyes and mind, ask yourself, "Do they detract from clarity?" If they do, take them out.

5.5

DECLARATION OF INDEPENDENCE

Unanimously Adopted In Congress, July 4, 1776, in Philadelphia, PA

When, in the course of human events, it becomes necessary for one people to dissolve the political bands which have connected them with another, and to assume among the powers of the earth, the separate and equal station to which the Laws of Nature and of Nature's God entitles them, a decent respect to the opinions of mankind requires that they should declare causes which impel them to the separation.

We hold these truths to be self-evident, that all men are created equal, that they are endowed by their Creator with certain unalienable Rights, that among these are Life, Liberty, and the pursuit of Happiness. That to secure these rights, Governments are instituted among Men, deriving their just powers from the consent of the governed. That whenever any Form of Government becomes destructive of these ends, it is the Right of the People to alter or to abolish it, and to institute new Government, laying its foundation on such principles and organizing its powers in such form, as to them shall seem most likely to effect their Safety and Happiness. Prudence, indeed, will dictate that Governments long established should not be changed for light and transient causes; and accordingly all experience hath shown, that mankind are more disposed to suffer, while evils are sufferable, than to right themselves by abolishing the forms to which they are accustomed. But when a long train of abuses and usurpations, pursuing invariably the same Object evinces a design to reduce them under absolute Despotism, it is their right, it is their duty, to throw off such Government, and to provide new guards for their future security. Such has been the patient sufferance of these Colonies; and such is not the necessity which constrains them to alter their former Systems of Government. The history of the present King of Great Britain is a history of repeated injuries and usurpations, all having in direct object the establishment of an absolute Tyranny over these States. To prove this, let Facts be submitted to a candid world.

He has refused his Assent to Laws, the most wholesome and necessary for the public good.

He has forbidden his Governors to pass Laws of immediate and pressing importance, unless suspended in their operation till his Assent should be obtained; and when so suspended, he has utterly neglected to attend to them.

He has refused to pass other Laws for the accommodation of large districts of people, unless those people would relinquish the right of Representation in the Legislature, a right inestimable to them and formidable to tyrants only.

He has called together legislative bodies at places unusual, uncomfortable, and distant from the depository of their public Records, for the sole purpose of fatiguing them into compliance with his measures.

He has dissolved Representative Houses repeatedly, for opposing with manly firmness his invasion on the rights of the people.

He has refused for a long time, after such dissolutions, to cause others to be elected; whereby the Legislative powers, incapable of Annihilation, have returned to the People at large for their exercise; the State remaining in the meantime exposed to all the dangers of invasion from without, and convulsions within.

He has endeavored to prevent the population of these States; for that purpose obstructing the Laws for Naturalization of Foreigners; refusing to pass others to encourage their migrations hither, and raising the conditions of new Appropriations of Lands

He has obstructed the Administration of Justice, by refusing his Assent to laws for establishing Judiciary Powers.

He has made Judges dependent on his Will alone, for the tenure of their offices, and the amount and payment of their salaries.

He has erected a multitude of New Offices, and sent hither swarms of Officers to harass our people, and eat out their substance.

He has kept among us, in times of peace, Standing Armies without the Consent of our Legislature.

He has affected to render the Military independence of and superior to the Civil power.

He has combined with others to subject us to a jurisdiction foreign to our constitution, and unacknowledged by our laws; giving his Assent to their Acts of pretended Legislation:

For quartering large bodies of armed troops among us:

For protecting them, by a mock Trial, from punishment for any Murders which they should commit on the Inhabitants of these States:

For cutting off our Trade with all parts of the world:

For imposing Taxes on us without our Consent:

For depriving us in many cases of the benefits of Trial by jury:

For transporting us beyond Seas to be tried for pretended offenses:

For abolishing the free System of English Laws in a neighboring Province, establishing therein an Arbitrary government, and enlarging its Boundaries so as to render it at once an example and fit instrument for introducing the same absolute rule into these Colonies:

For taking away our Charters, abolishing our most valuable Laws, and altering fundamentally the Forms of our Government:

For suspending our own Legislatures, and declaring themselves invested with power to legislate for us in all cases whatsoever.

He has abdicated Government here, by declaring us out of his Protection and waging War against us.

He has plundered our seas, ravaged our Coasts, burnt our towns, and destroyed the lives of our people.

He is at this time transporting large Armies of foreign Mercenaries to complete the works of death, desolation and tyranny, already begun with circumstances of Cruelty and perfidy scarcely paralleled in the most barbarous ages, and totally unworthy the Head of a civilized nation.

He has constrained our fellow-Citizens taken captive on the high Seas to bear Arms against their Country, to become the executioners of their friends and Brethren, or to fall themselves by their Hands.

He has excited domestic insurrections amongst us, and has endeavored to bring on the inhabitants of our frontiers, the merciless Indian Savages, whose known rule of warfare, is an undistinguished destruction of all ages, sexes and conditions.

In every stage of the Oppressions We have Petitioned for Redress in the most humble terms: Our repeated Petitions have been answered only by repeated injury. A Prince, whose character is thus marked by every act which may define a Tyrant, is unfit to be the ruler of a free people.

Nor have we been wanting in attention to our British brethren. We have warned them from time to time of attempts by their legislature to extend an unwarrantable jurisdiction over us. We have reminded them of the circumstances of our emigration and settlement here. We have appealed to their native justice and magnanimity, and we have conjured them by the ties of our common kindred to disavow these usurpations, which would inevitable interrupt our connections and correspondence. They, too, have been deaf to the voice of justice and of consanguinity. We must, therefore, acquiesce in the necessity, which denounces our Separation, and hold them, as we hold the rest of mankind; Enemies in War, in Peace Friends.

WE THEREFORE, the Representatives of the United States of America, in General Congress, Assembled, appealing to the Supreme Judge of the world for the rectitude of our intentions, do, in the Name, and by the authority of the good People of these Colonies, solemnly publish and declare, That these United Colonies, are and of Right ought to be free and independent States; that they are Absolved from all Allegiance to the British Crown, and that all political connection between them and the State of Great Britain is and ought to be totally dissolved; and that as Free and Independent States, they have full Power to levy War, conclude Peace, contract Alliance, establish Commerce, and to do all other Acts and Things which Independent States may of right do. And for the support of this Declaration, with a firm reliance on the protection of Divine Providence, we mutually pledge to each other our Lives, our Fortunes, and our sacred Honor.

duPont's Declaration

Sometimes you have to break ties with those who taught you and strike out on your own.

Since we believe that everyone is created equal; that a government should serve the people; that we all have the same rights, including life, liberty, happiness, and the right to institute new government when necessary for future security, we want to claim these rights and set up a new government that has a better chance of giving our people safety and happiness.

We didn't make this decision lightly. The King of Great Britain wants to establish a tyranny over us and we can't take the suffering any longer. Here's what he's done so far:

Refused to ratify laws necessary for the public good

Forbidden us to pass our own laws.

Refused to pass laws himself unless we would relinquish our right of representation

Called together our legislatures at unusual, uncomfortable, far-away places just to wear them down

Dissolved legislatures for opposing his invasion of rights and refused to elect others, leaving us exposed to invasion and domestic strife

Stopped people from coming to the States by obstructing naturalization

Refused to allow us to establish courts and appoint, discharge, and pay judges

Established new offices and sent swarms of new officers here to harass us

Left armies here in peacetime without our permission

Tried to make the military superior to civil law

Subjected us to people who have:

Quartered armed troops here

Protected themselves from punishment for murder

Cut off our trade with all parts of the world

Imposed taxes

Deprived us of trial by jury

Taken us to England to be tried for false offenses

Abolished English law in Canada and enlarged its boundaries, hoping to extend this control to us

Taken away our Charters, abolished our most valuable laws, and altered our government

Furthermore, the King has declared us out of his protection and waged war against us. He has plundered our seas, ravaged our coasts, burned our towns, and killed our people. He is now sending hired armies to complete the death, desolation, and tyranny already begun. He has captured our citizens on the high seas and forced them to fight against their country, killing their friends and dying themselves. He has caused rebellion among us and has tried to turn the Indians against us.

In every stage of these oppressions, we have petitioned for relief, to no avail. We've even appealed to the British people. We've often told them of attempts of their legislature to rule us and reminded them why we came here in the first place. We've appealed to their sense of justice and goodness, and to the ties of our common kindred. They haven't listened either.

We must, therefore, separate from Britain and hold the British people as we hold the rest of mankind: enemies in war, friends in peace.

So, the Representatives of the United States of America, in the name and by authority of the people, do solemnly decree that these United Colonies are free and independent states, and that all connection with Great Britain is totally dissolved.

For the support of this Declaration, with a firm reliance on God, we mutually pledge our lives, fortunes, and honor.

© 1990, M. Kay duPont, duPont and Disend Inc.
2137 Mt. Vernon Road, Atlanta, GA 30338

WORDY TO CONCISE:

WORDY	CONCISE
a large number of	many
ahead of schedule	early
and so as a result	thus
nine in number	nine
keep in mind the fact	remember
call a halt	stop
to a greater degree	more
without further delay	now
made an approach to	approached
give rise to	cause
is in possession of	has
am in the process of	am
at any early date, in the near future	soon
by the name of	named
during the time that	while, when
had occasion to be	was
in advance of this date, prior to	before
made a statement saying	said
render assistance, be of assistance	help
take action on the issue	act, take action, do
was of the opinion	thought
make reference to	refer
take corrective action	correct
are in receipt of	have
have under consideration	considering
give consideration to	consider
in view of the fact that, owing to the fact that, due to the fact that	because, since
at this present and current point in time	now
the majority of	most
for the purpose of	for, because, to
in the event that	if
advise us as to	let us know
pending our receipt of	when we receive
with respect to	about, as to

will you be so kind as to, we would like you to	please
the undersigned	I, me
is not in a position to	can't
am of the opinion that	think
in due course of time	soon
I wish to state, I want to thank	---(just do it!)
in spite of the fact that	although
in the neighborhood of	about, approximately
in addition, plus	and, also, too
convened	met
was concluded with alacrity	ended quickly

"Play it again, Sam."

Most meanings: *In English, the record for the word with the most meanings goes to <u>set</u>, which has—get set!—58 noun uses, 126 verbal uses, and 10 uses as a participial adjective—a total of 194 definitions!*

REDUNDANCIES TO AVOID

(adhesive) tape
AM (in the morning)
(a) myriad (of) sources
(absolute) guarantee
(absolutely) essential, necessary, sure
(actual) experience
add (an additional)
(advance) planning, warning
(advance) reservations
all meet (together)
alongside (of)
(already) existing
(and) moreover
(as) for example
ask (a question)
(as to) whether
(as) yet
(at a) later (date)
(at) about
(at a time) when
at (the) present (time)
at some time (to come)
(audible) sound
(awkward) predicament
(baby) boy was born
bald (headed)
(basic) fundamentals
blend (together)
(bolt of) lightning
bouquet (of flowers)
(brief) moment
burn (down) (up)
but (however) (nevertheless)
cancel (out)
(chief) protagonist
climb (up)
(close) proximity, scrutiny
(cold) facts
collaborate, combine (together)
commute (back and forth)
(complete) monopoly
(completely) filled, empty
(completely) surround, eliminate,
(completely) destroy
consensus (of opinion)
continue (on)

(continue to) remain
(current) fad, trend
(currently) being
dates (back)
(definite) decision
descend (down)
(different) kinds
(difficult) dilemma
(direct) confrontation
(distance of) ten yards
dive, drop, dwindle (down)
do (over) again
during (the course of)
each (and every) (one)
earlier (in time)
either (and/or both)
(empty) space
enclosed (herewith please find)
(end) result
enter (in)
equal (to one another)
eradicate (completely)
(established) fact
estimated at (about)
estimated (roughly) at
(every) now and then
(exactly) identical
(exact) opposites
face (up to)
(false) pretenses
(fatal) slayings
(fellow) classmates
few (in number)
filled (to capacity)
(finally) ended
(final) outcome
(first) began
first (of all) (and foremost)
fix (up)
follow (after)
for (a period of) 10 days
(foreign) imports
forever (and ever)
(forseeable) future
(free) gift, pass
(future) plans

gather (together)
(general) consensus (of opinion)
(general) conclusion, custom
(general) public, rule
(glowing) ember
golden (wedding) anniversary
(grand) total
(guest) speaker
had done (previously)
(hard) facts
heat (up)
(hostile) antagonist
(hot) water heater
impeach (from office)
I (myself) (personally)
indicted (on a charge)
(integral) part
(in order) to
introduced (a new)
introduced (for the first time)
(invited) guests
(in the process of)
is (now) pending
join (together)
(just) exactly, recently
kneel (down)
last (of all)
lift (up)
(live) band
(local) residents
look back (in retrospect)
lose (out)
(major) breakthrough
(mass) media
may (possibly)
mean it (sincerely)
(mental) telepathy
merged, meshed (together)
midnight (on the night of)
(midway) between
might (possibly)
mix (together)
(month of) June
(mutual) cooperation
my (personal) opinion
(native) habitat
(natural) instinct
(necessary) requirements
never (at any time) (before)
(new) beginning, bride, baby

(new) construction, innovation
(new) record, recruit
none (at all)
(null and) void
off (of)
(official) business
(old) adage, cliche
(old) pioneer, proverb
(one and) the same
(originally) created
over (and done with)
(over) exaggerate
over (with)
(pair of) twins
(partially) damaged, destroyed
(passing) fad
(past) experience, history
(past) memories, records
permeate (throughout)
penetrate (into)
(perfect) ideal
period (of time)
(personal) friendship, opinion
(pitch) black
pizza (pie)
plan (ahead) (of action)
(possibly) might
postponed (until later)
(pre)plan, record
(present) incumbent
probed (into)
proceed (ahead)
protest (against)
protrude (out)
(rate of) speed
recur (again)
refer, revert, reflect, reply
(back)
relic (of the past)
remember (in my mind)
repeat, redo (again)
reason was (because)
reason (why)
rise (to your feet)
(rustic) country
(same) identical
(separate) entities
separate (and distinct)
share (together)
since (the time when)

skipped (over)
slow (down)
soaked (to the skin)
spell out (in detail)
stacked (together)
start (out)
started (off) with
(still) remains, persists
(suddenly) collapsed, exploded
sufficient (enough)
(sum) total
summer (season)
(sworn) affidavit
talking (out loud)
(temporary) reprieve
together (at the same time)
(toxic) poison

(true) fact
(twelve o'clock) noon, midnight
(two) both
undergraduate (student)
(underground) subway
(unexpected) surprise
(unintentional) mistake
until (such a time as)
(usual) custom
various (and different)
visible (to the eye)
(when and) if
whether (or not)
within (the course of)
written (down)
(year of) 1990
(young) child

How clear is your writing?

Find a letter you've written and evaluate it based on this readability scale. Use only the first 100 words. First, count the pronouns (See Chapter 8) and circle the appropriate number in Column A. Next, count the average number of words in your sentences and circle the appropriate number in Column C. Draw a line between the circles. Your clarity level is the one in Column B that the line touches. If you need to move up or down Column B a little to make it work, move down. If your clarity level is below "Probable," you need to work on your writing.

Pronouns Per 100 Words	Probability of Being Misunderstood	Average Words Per Sentence
19 or more	Extremely improbable	9 or fewer
9-18	Highly improbable	10-15
5-17	Probable	16-19
3-5	Highly probable	20-26
0-2	Virtually certain	30 or more

Sixteen Pointers For Style

(1) Write the way you speak. Within reason, of course. Don't put in the slang, filler phrases, colloquialisms, and non-existent words that we use in speech. But do put in contractions, the reader's name, personal pronouns, simple words. Start your sentences with conjunctions occasionally, and end them with prepositions once in a while. Split your infinitives. Your readers will appreciate your honest style much more than an affected, pompous, English literature-type style. Don't change your style just because you're facing a typewriter. But don't use bad grammar either. Write the way you would speak to an educated person in an important situation.

(2) Keep it simple. Simple, preferably short, sentences make all communication—speeches, reports, letters—more understandable. The emphasis of a sentence should lie not in its length, but in its words. The longer your sentences, the longer your letter; the longer your letter, the less likely it is to be read. It's not easy to write simply; it's much easier to be complex or to ramble. But once you get the hang of it, it's a lot more fun, a lot quicker, and a lot less energy-consuming. Remember Kay's Rule of Max (Page 4.8).

(3) Present your points in logical order. Logical organization is basic to clarity. The thoughts in a letter should proceed in logical sequence, one flowing into another from start to finish, in a sequence that's easy for the reader's mind to absorb. This principle applies to letters, paragraphs, sentences, even phrases.

How do you achieve such a sequence? By thinking your letter out step by step before you write it—or before you do the second draft. The clarity of a letter is often improved by reversing the sequence of paragraphs. A paragraph may be made clearer by changing the sequence of sentences; a sentence, by changing the order of phrases; a phrase, by varying the order of words. Ideas should fit on top of one another like building blocks, but be sure you get the bottom blocks in first.

(4) Tell the readers what your letter is about in the first paragraph. Don't keep your readers guessing; they're as busy as you are. Reading a letter shouldn't be a chore—any more than writing one. Watch those first five or six words. If they are strong and friendly, the other words will tend to follow the same pattern.

Your opening words make or break your message. To a large extent, they determine the mood or tone of your letter. It's hard to make your reader believe you're friendly if your opening is cold. It's always acceptable to open with *Thank you for...* and to close with *Thank you again for....* Use a short opening sentence, get to the point, and stick to the point.

(5) Ask for what you want. That's the best way I know to <u>get</u> what you want. If you beat around the bush in your correspondence, your readers will probably procrastinate, because it just won't seem too important. We've become a nation of indirect writers who, oddly, wonder why our instructions are not followed or our letters answered.

If I wrote you a memo and, somewhere in the last paragraph, I said, *"I'm enclosing the year-end report for your review,"* would you read it? Probably not. What if the first sentences of my memo said, *"Here's the year-end report. Please read this and call me before Tuesday,"* would you read it now? You'd better! Ask for what you want and you'll probably get it.

There's one catch, however: you have to <u>know</u> what you want before you begin to write. Start with a clear, well-defined purpose that you can express in one sentence: *I want an answer by next Tuesday.* List all the major points you want to get across—in one simple sentence each, in their order of importance.

(6) Be positive. Sentences should be written in a positive tone whenever possible. We all prefer to hear what <u>is</u> rather than what <u>is</u> <u>not</u>, so the reader will be more receptive to what you have to say. Also, by writing in the negative, you run the risk of generating a negative response; by writing in the positive, you are more likely to get a positive response. Look for sentences from which you can cut the negative:

Negative: *The answer **does not lie** with carelessness or incompetence.*

Better: *The answer **lies in** having enough people to do the job.*

Negative: *Because of the difficulty in our inventory department, we will not be able to complete your repair this month.*

Better: *We're happy to tell you that your repair will be completed by August 1. We apologize for the delay.*

Negative: *We can't incorporate all the specified design features without increasing the unit size.*

Better: *To provide the specified design features, we have increased the unit size.*

If you can help it, don't tell readers your problems and don't tell them what you <u>can't</u> do. Tell them what you <u>can</u> do.

(7) Use the active voice. Active voice is when <u>you</u> <u>do</u> something, passive voice is when something <u>is</u> <u>done</u> to you. Active construction is always preferable to passive, and you should use the active voice is often as possible. Let your subject do to your object (Subject, Verb, Object), rather than having your object be done to by your subject (Verb, Object, Subject). Invariably, this produces a shorter, livelier, more personable sentence. Because passive verbs are impersonal and indirect, passive sentence structure is usually weak and awkward, and often requires a lot of unnecessary words and prepositional phrases that result in a dull sentence.

> *Pac-Man **was hit** right on his little yellow head by Kay.* (Passive, 11 words)

> *Kay **hit** Pac-Man right on his little yellow head.* (Active, 9 words)

> *The cherry tree **was chopped** down by George Washington.* (Passive, 9 words)

> *George Washington **chopped** down the cherry tree.* (Active, 7 words)

> *Your cooperation **will be appreciated.*** (Passive, 7 words—you must include the implied *by whom.)*

> *We **will appreciate** your cooperation.* (Active, 5 words)

Passive sentences tend to drag; active sentences are bold and direct. The most important characteristic of life is movement, and we can show this in our writing by using active words.

(8) Use your sense of humor. That's a refreshing, nice surprise anytime—in <u>any</u> letter.

5.17

(9) Avoid jargon. Don't use words, expressions, or phrases known only to people with specific knowledge or interests, and don't write on a level higher than your reader's knowledge. For example, a speech writer for President Franklin D. Roosevelt wrote, "We are endeavoring to construct a more inclusive society." F.D.R. changed it to, "We're going to make a country in which no one is left out." Today's politicians should take lessons from Mr. Roosevelt.

(10) Avoid colloquialisms, cliches, hyperboles, euphemisms, outdated language. If you do use a colloquialism or a slang word or phrase, simply use it; don't exaggerate it verbally or draw attention to it by enclosing it in quotation marks in your written material. To do so is to be condescending. And, technically, quotation marks around a word or phrase serve to reverse your meaning. So if you say that your restaurant serves "fine" food, you're really saying that the food isn't really so good.

Some slang contributes to the vitality of the language, but reserve it for oral use. Even in your speech, you should try to avoid such slang expressions as:

You Know: I believe this phrase has been unleashed on us to stifle our natural thinking processes. (What bothers me most is that some people just agree with these mindless stutterings, just as if the speaker had completed a sentence and they understood it!) *You know what I mean* and simply *I mean* are also problems.

Gonna/Gotta: Haphazard contractions for *going to*. These crazy words are just *gonna* take over the world. I've just *gotta* get the point across that these words are not a contraction for anything.

Irregardless: Still considered very poor English by the experts and most of the world. It actually negates itself twice: *Ir* and *less* are both negative affixes. Use *regardless.*

Enthused: A back-formation from the word *enthusiastic*. This word is considered substandard by most. Use *enthusiastic*.

Authored: The word *author* is a noun, and nouns don't have tenses. Use *wrote.*

Ain't: Still considered substandard usage. Use *are not* or *am not.*

Cliches: The word *cliche* comes from the French *cliches*, meaning *to stereotype*, which means *to make a printing plate from a matrix or mold taken from set type*. The idea is of a hard and fixed thing, and that describes some qualities of a cliche. Other qualities are triteness and boredom. Cliches are a lazy person's attempt at figurative speaking. Avoid such phrases as:

Too funny for words	*At a loss for words*
No sooner said than done	*Hard as a rock*
Last but not least	*It stands to reason*
Where's the beef?	*The bottom line*

Hyperboles: Expressions we use when we want to exaggerate. Most of them are *hard to swallow*. Avoid phrases like:

Swims like a rock	*Almost died laughing*
Could eat a horse	*Dead tired*
Dying for a drink	*Literally buried in work*
Madly in love	*Can't wait to see you*
Worked my fingers	*Scared to death*
to the bone	*Mad as an old wet hen*

Euphemisms: Expressions used to avoid disagreeable subjects. As former U.S. Senator Everett Dirksen (R-IL) once said, "A euphemism is something that seems like what it ain't." Some euphemisms, of course, come from our wish to soften a blow or to not offend, but many are the result of a false sense of prudery or lack of imagination. For instance, we are no longer born, we arrive as *little blessings in the home*. We don't sweat, we *perspire*. We aren't poor people—we're the *underprivileged minority*. We have no young criminals, only *juvenile delinquents*. We never receive pay relief or make money, we receive *unemployment compensation* or *generate revenue*. Garbage collectors have become *sanitation engineers*, and housekeepers have become *domestic engineers*. We don't even get fired or die anymore—we *experience negative career development* and *pass away*. Whether I die or pass away, the fact remains that I am dead, and no euphemism is going to help me.

Outdated language: Many words and phrases appear in our correspondence that are just outdated. These words separate the reader and writer with a pompous barrier rather than creating a sense of authority.

<u>Old Fashioned</u>	<u>Use</u>
amid/amidst/amongst	in, among
unto	to
upon	on

angst	anxiety
arcane	hidden, secret
kempt	neat, tidy, kept
nocuous	harmful, poisonous, toxic
ept	apt, able
beauteous	beautiful
firstly	first
thusly	so
whence	where, when
ye	you
nevertheless	anyway, but
one	you
moreover	and

(11) Use nonsexist language. Not only are expressions such as *the working man* outdated, they also perpetuate the myths that were responsible for keeping women out of positions of authority for so long. It's time to make a conscious effort to strip our language of words and expressions that don't express equality. Here's a list of outdated expressions and suggestions for nonsexist replacements:

<u>Old Form</u>	<u>New Form</u>
authoress, poetess	author, poet
businessmen	businesspeople
chairman	chairperson, chair
coeds	students
Congressman	member of Congress, representative, Congressperson
employees and their wives	employees and their spouses
fellow worker	coworker
firemen, policemen	fire fighters, police officers
gal friday	office worker, assistant, secretary
girl	woman
he/she	they

housewives	homemakers
lady doctor, lady lawyer	doctor, lawyer
male nurse, male secretary	nurse, secretary
mailmen, postmen	postal workers, mail carriers
man and wife	man and woman, husband and wife
man hours	work hours
man in the street	average person
mankind	people, humanity, human race, human beings
man-made	synthetic, manufactured, constructed, hand-made
manpower	work force
repairmen, foremen	repairers, supervisors
salesmen	salespeople, sales representatives
stewardess, steward	flight attendant
working man	working person, worker, employee

(12) Use parallel elements. Writing and speaking demand rhythm, just like music and dancing. And, to have rhythm, a sentence must balance. *I came, I saw, I conquered*—three simple sentences in one, three balanced parts of a whole. Parallelism is the way we make our sentences balance evenly.

Of course, not every parallel structure is so memorable, but most sentences with multiple parts will have a pendulum, or a pivot point, from which all the elements should balance evenly.

For instance: *Most students either work a second job, get money from home, or their spouses work.*

The first two items are all right—students *work* and students *get*—but students *their spouses work*? It makes no sense and is grammatically unsound. It should be *have working spouses* or *make their spouses work,* or a similar construction beginning with a verb. Verbs must be parallel with verbs.

5.22

students
work · get · have

Be especially careful when using an article as your pivot point. You must make sure that the article can hold both nouns.

We need a horse and an apple.

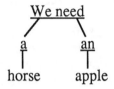

We need
a · an
horse · apple

Parallelism is especially important when we begin an outline or series with a participle: *My child enjoys dating, eating, swimming, and to sleep.*

If the first word of your series ends with **_ing_**, so should all of them: *My child enjoys swimming, dating, eating, and **sleeping**.*

Enumerations have an especially critical need for parallelism:

You will learn the following things from this book:

(1) Agreement of verbs
(2) Letter styles
(3) Writing techniques
(4) To properly spell words

The first three items are nouns, but the fourth is an infinitive, which is a verb. So it should be **_"Spelling"_** or some other noun construction. (You could also change the other three elements to infinitives, but that sounds like unnecessary work.)

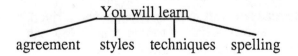

You will learn
agreement · styles · techniques · spelling

5.23

Sentences must also be parallel in voice:

*After this lesson **is studied*** (passive),
*you **will understand** parallelism* (active).

It would be better to write:

*After **you study** this lesson* (active),
*you **will understand** parallelism* (active).

Parallelism, then, means expressing ideas in parallel grammatical forms. The key is consistency. If the first of a series of ideas is expressed as a noun, a verb, an adjective, or a phrase, then the second, third, and fourth ideas should be presented in the same grammatical form. Adjective must follow adjective, noun must follow noun, active must follow active, etc. Put simply, you can't compare <u>unlike</u> units.

Parallelism helps your reader quickly and clearly understand the proper relationship of ideas, and should be strictly adhered to.

(13) Don't let your participles dangle. A participle is simply a verb form that ends in *ing*. It's often used as the first word of a modifying phrase: **Having *nothing else to do, I ate an entire chocolate cake.***

A participle dangles when it's incorrectly placed in the sentence and appears to modify something it doesn't: ***Sitting on my mother's lap, the circus was more enjoyable.*** Doesn't that sound like the *circus* was sitting on my mother's lap? That's a dangling participle.

Consider the sentence: ***On arriving at the airport, my friends met me at the gate.*** <u>Who</u> arrived at the airport? The way the sentence reads now, it was my <u>friends</u> who arrived, because the participle phrase is adjacent to that noun. How can you modify <u>I</u> if <u>I</u> doesn't even appear in the sentence?

This problem can easily be solved by the skeleton rule: (1) head (who/what), (2) body (did/does/do what), (3) feet (to whom/ what), (4) fluff (when, where, why, how?) (See Chapter 4).

Shoe. Reprinted by permission: Tribune Media Services

Even if you put some fluff up front, make sure your head comes before your feet:

> **(when)** *On arriving at the airport,*
> **(who)** *I* **(did what)** *met* **(to whom)** *my friends* **(where)**
> *at the gate.*

Of course your best structure is really:

> **(who)** *I* **(did what)** *met* **(to whom)** *my friends* **(where)**
> *at the airport* **(when)** *when I arrived.*

Participles aren't the only modifiers that dangle. Adjectives and adverbs can dangle too. Just as modifiers can add so much to our sentences, so they can detract if they're not the right words or if they're in the wrong places. Single modifiers should be adjacent to, and preferably in front of, what they modify; modifying phrases follow the skeleton rule.

Let's look at some examples and possible solutions:

Covered in chocolate, you can really enjoy ice cream.

> **Better:** (**who**) *Ice cream* (**does what**) *is really enjoyable* (**how**) *covered in chocolate.*

> **Better still:** *You can really enjoy chocolate-covered ice cream.*

The fire was extinguished before any damage could be done by the fire department.

> **Better:** (**who**) *The fire department* (**did what**) *extinguished* (**to whom**) *the fire* (**when**) *before any damage could be done.*

> **Better still:** *The fire department extinguished the fire before it could do any damage.*

The lecturer talked during the banquet of poisonous snakes.

> **Better:** (**when**) *During the banquet,* (**who**) *the lecturer* (**did what**) *talked* (**how**) *of poisonous snakes.*

> **Better still:** *The lecturer talked of poisonous snakes during the banquet.*

5.26

Being in a dilapidated condition, I bought the house cheaply.

Better: (who) *I* (did what) *bought* (to whom) *the house* (how) *cheaply* (why) *because of its dilapidated condition.*

Better still: *I cheaply bought the dilapidated house.*

As a mother of five, my ironing board is always busy.

Better: (how) *As a mother of five,* (who) *I* (do what) *am always busy* (how) *ironing.*

Better still: *Because I have five children, I am always ironing.*

Don't let your modifiers dangle just anywhere in a sentence they happen to fall. Make sure they relate to the word they are supposed to relate to. Your sentence structure will be more effective, and you'll be more easily understood.

(14) Distinguish opinions from facts. Your opinions may be the most intelligent in town, but they're not <u>facts</u>. You owe it to your readers to let them know which is which. Be honest and don't exaggerate. It'll get you further in the long run.

(15) Use statements, not questions. Although it's true that questions are sometimes important to keep your readers interested, awake, and involved, many questions will usually bog your message down. Most of the questions we ask in letters don't need answers anyway. If you don't really want a specific answer, why ask the question?

(16) Sum up and shut up. The last paragraph should tell your readers exactly what you want them to do—or what <u>you're</u> going to do: *May I have an appointment?* OR *I'll call you next Tuesday.* Remember that *"Thank you for..."* is a good opening for any letter. *"Thank you again for..."* is a good closing for any letter.

IT'S HARD TO SOAR WITH EAGLES IF YOU WRITE LIKE A TURKEY!

CHAPTER 6: SPELLING

Why should we be so careful with our spelling?

Because correct spelling is one of the marks of an educated and efficient professional, no matter what your line of business. For that reason, you shouldn't permit yourself to misspell words even in your personal correspondence. Misspelling one word can actually create a new word that means something entirely different (like prescribe and proscribe).

How can we learn to spell better?

Spelling is not difficult, especially with those 12-pound cheat sheets most of us keep on our desks. The dictionary is a writer's best friend and should be updated at least every five years. Choose a dictionary you trust, and make sure you get the latest edition. See the bibliography for recommendations.

The best way to learn to spell is to keep a list in the front of your dictionary. Every time you look up a word, write it on the list. Not only will writing it down help enforce the correct spelling in your memory, it will also save time when you need to look it up again. (Don't we seem to look up the same words over and over?) The added incentive of seeing that you have already looked it up also makes it easier to remember. This list will be invaluable to you if you have trouble with spelling.

Some people actually ask me, "But how can I find a word in the dictionary when I don't know how to spell it in the first place?" I guess that's not as silly as it sounds, but there is an easier way to figure it out than going through the dictionary page by page. <u>Think</u> about the word. Really think about how it sounds. Then pronounce it out loud, by exaggerated syllables, and picture the word as you say it. Say the word slowly <u>before</u> you try to spell it, <u>as</u> you spell it and again <u>after</u> you spell it, and picture the word as you say it: It's *athlete*, not *athelete*; *cruel*; not *crule*, *interested*, not *interested*; *project*, not *projeck*.

Sometimes, of course, sounds do get lost in pronunciation. George Bernard Shaw once proved this by spelling *fish* this way: *ghoti*. He used the *f* as it sounds in *enough*, the *i* as it sounds in *women*, and the *sh* as it sounds in *fiction*.

You can help yourself solve the problem posed by weak sounds by thinking of another word in the same family. Think of *re-late* and you should have no trouble with *relative*. Think of *humor* and you shouldn't misspell *humorous*. Think of *victor* and you won't misspell *victorious*.

Also, if you can associate words with their origin, or with mnemonics (memory tricks), you'll have the spelling problem conquered. I always had trouble with the word *weird* until I finally realized that the correct way to spell it is weird in itself, so I always choose the spelling that looks wrong.

If you really can't figure out the first syllable, look up another word that means about the same thing. For instance, if you couldn't spell *feline*, you could look up *cat*.

Another excellent way to ease your spelling woes is to renew your knowledge of prefixes and suffixes. If you know that *anti* means *against*, you should have no trouble with **anti**trust** and **anti**war** and **anti**biotic**. If you know that *ante* means *before*, you should be able to spell **ante**cedent** and **ante**date** and **ante**room**.

Just remember these rules when using prefixes and suffixes (see also Chapter 9):

(1) Most common prefixes and suffixes join solidly to a full base word, with no break or hyphen and no addition or deletion of letters.

(2) Never use a hyphen with a suffix (except *like* when attached to a word ending in *l*).

(3) Use a hyphen with a prefix <u>only</u> when:

- The prefix is added to a capitalized word (***un-Southern***)

- The prefix is added to a number (***pre-1990***)

- Deleting the hyphen would cause confusion with another existing word (***re-create/recreate, co-op/coop, re-sign/resign***)

- The prefix is *ex* (meaning former), *self*, or *all*.

Here's a partial list of prefixes and suffixes and their meanings:

COMMON PREFIXES

a, ab, abs,: from, away from
ac, ad, of, ag, al, an, ap, at: to, at, toward, thoroughly
ambi: both, around, on both sides
an: not, without
ante: before, ahead of
anti: against, opposite
be: around, completely off, about, make, furnish with
bi: two, every two times, double, doubly
circum: around
co, cog, col, com, con, cor: with, together
contra, conto: against, opposed to
de: off, away, freeing from, depriving of, completely
di: two-fold
di, dif, dis: from, not, apart

dis: not
e, ec, ef, ex: out of, off, from, without, thoroughly
en, em: in, into, toward
eph, epi: over, upon
equi: equally
extra: beyond, outside
eu: good, well, advantageous
extro: outward
ig, il, im, in, ir: not
il, im, in, ir: into, in, toward
inter: between, among
intra: within, in the interior
mis: wrong, ill, bad, incorrectly
multi: many
non: not
over: too much
per: through, by means of, thoroughly
peri: around
poly: many
post: after
pre: before, prior to
pro: for, forward, in favor of, toward the front
psuedo: false, fictitious
re, red: back, backward
retro: back, again
se: aside, apart, without
self: by one's self (*often best omitted*)
semi: half
sub, suc, suf, sug, sum, sup, sur, sus: under
super, supra: above, higher, over, beyond the usual
syl, sym, syn: along with, like, together
tri: three
ultra: excessively, exceedingly, beyond
un: not, without, removed
under: too little

COMMON SUFFIXES

able, ible, ble: worthy of being, fit to be, capable of being (*able* usually attaches to a complete word)

ability: capable of

ac, ic: pertaining to, consisting of, in the nature of, like, belonging

acy: state or quality of being

an: belonging to, pertaining to

ance, ancy, ence, ency: state, act, quality, process, being

  ant, ent: one who, tending toward

ar, ary: belonging to, relating to, like

ar, er, or: one who

ate: act, condition of being, having function of, possessing

ation, ion, ition: state, condition, process of being

cle, cule: small

cy: state, quality, office, rank

ee: one to whom an act is done or a right is granted

eer: one who conducts, manages, or produces

er: a person or thing doing something, a comparative degree between two items

ery, ry: character, behavior, conduct, art, trade, occupation, place where something is done

esque: in the manner or style

est: superlative degree between three or more items

ette: small

fic: causing

fold: multiplied by

ful: abounding in, characterized by, full of

gamy: marriage

ion: action

ious: having quality of

ous: having quality of

wise: in the manner of (*usually best omitted*)

COMPOUNDS--WITH OR WITHOUT A HYPHEN?*

(Verbs are not listed. As a rule, verbs don't have hyphens.)

above-mentioned
  (formal usage only)
above ground
air-conditioned
air conditioner
airfare/airplane/airline
all-out
all right
a lot
antitrust
attorney at law
audiovisual
biannual
bona fide
bookstore/bookshop
boyfriend/girlfriend
breakdown
break-even
break-in
businessperson
businesswoman
bylaws
byproduct
changeover
checkbook
checkout
checkpoint
checkup
close out
coinsure
coworker
cross-reference
cutoff
database/databank
double-edged
double talk

drugstore
even-tempered
everyday (adj. only)
everywhere
first-class
firsthand
follow-through
follow-up
freelance
free-standing
full-time
go-ahead
goodbye
goodwill
high school
homeowner
hometown
hopefully
household
inasmuch as
inattentive
in-depth
insofar as
interoffice
interstate
intrastate
knockout (adj. and
  noun)
know-how
lawsuit
leasehold
letterhead
lifelong
lifestyle
long-distance
long-standing

long-term
makeshift
makeup
markup/markdown
middle age
middle-aged
middleman
millimeter
minicomputer
newsworthy
nonindependent
nonoperational
nonpayment
nonprofit
nonrecurring
nontaxable
offset
one-half (adj.)
one half (noun)
outset
overall
overpayment
overstock
part-time
passbook
past-due
payday
payroll
Pegboard
per capita
percent
photocopy
postdated
post office
profit-sharing
pro rata

* According to *Webster's New World Dictionary, Third College Edition,*
Simon & Schuster, Inc., 1988.

6.6

prorated
rain check
reelection
reemphasis
reevaluation
right of way
run-down (adj.)
runners-up
safekeeping
self-explanatory
semiannual

setback
setup
short-term
shutdown
signboard
so-called
stockholder
storeroom
storewide
sublease
tax-free/tax-exempt

teenage
time-consuming
time frame
timetable
trademark
twenty-seven
upcoming
updated
upgraded
up-to-date (adj.)

If you're familiar with the words you use, you'll probably
spell them correctly—and you shouldn't be using words
you're unfamiliar with anyway.

HOW *DO* WE SPELL THOSE TRICKY WORDS?

abbreviate
absence
abundance
accelerator
accessible
accommodate
accumulate
achieve
acknowledgment
acquaintance
admissible
advantageous
adviser
affidavit
afterward
aging
airfare
allegiance
allotment
allotted
all right
ambience
analysis
analyze
ancient
ancillary
anoint
anonymous
apologize
apparatus
appearance
apropos
arrangement
assimilate
assistance
assurance
athlete
attendance
authoritative
auxiliary
backward
bankruptcy
believable
beneficiary

benefited
benevolent
blond
bookkeeper
bulletin
bureau
buses/busing/bused
caffeine
calendar
camaraderie
canceled
cancellation
category
catalog
ceiling
cemetery
center
changeable
characteristic
chiefly
clientele
collateral
collectible
colonel
column
commission
commitment
committee
comparative
competence
competitive
concede
conceivable
confidential
congratulate
conscientious
consensus
corps
courteous
cozy
criticism
cupfuls
cylinder
database

deceive
defendant
definitely
desirable
despair
dependent
desperate
development
dialog
dilemma
discernible
diligent
disastrous
discernible
discrepancy
dissatisfied
earnest
echelon
embarrass
employee
en route
envelope
epitomize
erratic
erroneous
essence
exaggerate
excerpt
exemption
exhibition
exhilarate
existence
exorbitant
extraordinary
exuberant
facetious
familiar
feasibility
February
fictitious
fierce
flexible
fluorescent
foreign

forfeit
fortunate
forty
fourth
freight
friend
gaiety
gauge
government
grammar
grateful
grievous
grievance
guarantee
harass
height
hindrance
holistic
humorous
hypocrisy
idiosyncrasy
illegible
inaccurate
inadvertent
incessant
incidentally
independent
indictment
indispensable
innuendo
inquiry
inundate
insistent
installment
interfered
irrelevant
irreparable
irresistible
irrevocable
itinerary
jeopardize
judgment
ketchup
khaki
knowledgeable

labeled
laid
leisure
lessor
liaison
license
lightning
likelihood
liquefy
loneliness
lying
maintenance
manageable
mandatory
maneuver
mediocre
memento
mileage
miniature
miscellaneous
mischievous
misspell
monotonous
mortgage
movable
narrative
necessary
negligible
neither
nickel
niece
ninety
noticeable
occasion
occurrence
often
omitted
overrun
paid
pamphlet
parallel
paraphernalia
pastime
payer
perceive

perilous
permanent
permissible
perseverance
personnel
pessimistic
pharmaceutical
phenomenon
Philippines
physician
picnicking
piece
plagiarize
plausible
pneumonia
poisonous
posthumous
potatoes
predominant
preferable
prerequisite
presence
prevalent
privilege
precede
predictable
procedure
proceed
proficient
programmed
prominent
pronunciation
propitious
pseudonym
psychology
publicly
quantitative
questioned
questionnaire
rapport
rarefy
receipt
receivable
recommend
recuperate

recurrence
referred
remembrance
repetition
reprieve
rescind
resistance
restaurant
reversible
rheumatism
rhythm
ridiculous
sacrilegious
salable
satellite
schedule
scissors
seize
separate
sergeant
siege
silhouette

similar
simultaneous
simplify
skeptical
sophomore
specialty
strategy
stupefy
succeed
succinct
superintendent
supersede
surprise
surveillance
synonymous
tariff
technician
temperament
temporarily
theater
thorough
through

toward
tranquility
transferable
transferred
truly
unanimity
unanimous
unnecessary
usable
usage
useful
vacuum
vague
versatile
vetoes
waiver
weird
wholly
withheld
yield
zeros

You should buy a new dictionary every five years.

CHAPTER 7: WORDS

The difference between the right word and the almost-right word is the difference between lightning and the lightning bug.

--Mark Twain

Using the wrong word in a sentence can hurt your image as badly as wearing two different colored shoes to a job interview. And there's often a big difference in small shades of meaning.

In *Alice in Wonderland*, Humpty Dumpty said, "When I use a word, it means just what I choose it to mean, neither more nor less. The question of words is which is to be master, that's all." That's not true in today's business world. You can't use a word incorrectly just because it sounds or *feels* better to you. The words must be masters of their own meanings if you are to be master of your message.

The way we use words is often inexact for several reasons: Many words have multiple meanings; there are many words in our language that are similar; we've become grammatically lazy and some words are easier to say than the proper ones.

Using the wrong word can lead to misunderstandings even quicker than using the right word incorrectly. You may know exactly what you mean to say, but are you confusing your readers by using the wrong word?

The Wonderful Words

Never let a thought shrivel and die
For want of a way to say it.
For English is a wonderful game
And all of us can play it.
All you do is match the words
To the brightest thought in your head
So they come out clear and true
And beautifully groomed and fed.

Words are the food and dress of thought—
They give it body and swing,
And everyone's longing today to hear
Some fresh and beautiful thing.
But only words can free a thought
From its prison behind your eyes.
Maybe your mind is holding
A marvelous new surprise!

What are some of these confusing words and how can we remember the difference?

For a more complete list, see *Just Words*, a new book of confusing words by M. Kay duPont, CSP.

A/AN: In the earliest stages of the American language, there was no such article as **a**. But it required too much effort to say *an* great day, *an* friendly horse. So speakers tended to slur the **an** (as we still slur many of our words), and **a** came into the American language. For some reason, Americans held on to *an hotel* and *an university* for many years, but these too have passed into the common rule: Use **a** before a consonant sound and **an** before a vowel sound. Since americans usually pronounce their h's, a is proper with most h words, The only American h words that take **an** today are *heir, hour, honest, honor, herb*, and variants of these.

A/PER: Interchangeable.

ABOUT/AROUND: **Around** means surrounding, in every direction. **About** means near, nearly, on all sides of, regarding. **About** *30 people came to the party. Things are really hectic* around *here.*

ACCEPTANCE/ACCEPTATION: **Acceptance** is an approval; an acceptability; a belief in; a bill of exchange that has been accepted for payment; and, in law, an act by which you accept an obligation. An **acceptation** is the generally accepted meaning of a word or expression. These definitions are **acceptations.**

ACKNOWLEDGE/ADMIT/ALLOW: All mean to concede or make a disclosure, but **allow** takes more words: you can **admit** *a mistake* or **acknowledge** *a mistake* or **allow** *that you have made a mistake.* **Acknowledge** is preferable when referring to a statement made reluctantly, especially one previously denied, and **admit** suggests that you were under some pressure. *To* is unnecessary with **admit.**

ACQUIRE: See Get.

ACT/ACTION: Synonymous as nouns.

AD HOC/STANDING: An **ad hoc** committee is elected or appointed to complete a single assignment. A **standing** committee meets regularly and handles all ongoing assignments within its defined authority.

ADDENDUM/ADDENDA: An **addendum** is an addition and is specifically applied to an appendix of, or supplement to, printed material. It is always singular. The standard plural is **addenda**, although most authorities no longer consider **addendums** incorrect.

ADDICTED/DEVOTED: **Addicted** implies an undesirable sense of attachment. **Devoted** implies a beneficial attachment, a dedication. **Devoted *to children*, addicted *to drugs*.**

ADDITIONAL/FURTHER: Both mean more, but **additional** has the sense of quantity; it's closer to *and*. **Further** has the sense of distance, time, degree. *If you need* **additional** *information, please call.*

ADDUCE/DEDUCE: **Adduce** means to cite as evidence that is conclusive or persuasive, to present as an example: *The woman* adduced *three reasons for her decision*. **Deduce** means to infer, to conclude from something assumed or known: *The jury* deduced *that the witness was lying*.

ADHERE/COHERE: An object **adheres** to another through the use of an outside force (glue, a cause, a religion, etc.). An object **coheres** because of natural forces: *Each part of the presentation* cohered *with the facts.*

ADMISSION/ADMITTANCE: In nonelectrical use, **admittance** means only permission or right to enter. **Admission** also means the fee paid to enter; a granting of the truth; and acknowledging of a crime, fault, etc.; and the thing confessed. So your **admission** (fee) will gain you either **admittance** or **admission.** Your statement is always **admission.**

ADMIT: See Acknowledge.

ADOPTED/ADOPTIVE: If you are legally taken in by others, you are **adopted.** The ones who took you in are **adoptive.**

ADVANCE/ADVANCEMENT: Interchangeable in the noun sense of a moving forward, an improvement.

ADVICE/ADVISE: **Advice** is a noun. **Advise** is a verb (remember _s_ for **say**). When you give suggestions, you **advise.** The suggestions themselves are the **advice.**

AFFECT/EFFECT: As a verb, **affect** has four meanings, all starting with _a_ to help your memory.

(1) Act on: *That man* **affects** *her emotionally every time she sees him.*

(2) Assume: *Sometimes she* affects *a Southern accent just for fun.*

(3) Adopt: *The manager of our store decided to* affect *the same window display as the other store.*

(4) Alter: *The new company policy will* affect *the work schedule.*

Affect is not used as a noun in everyday language, but it may be used as a noun in psychological terminology to mean the emotional part of the human psyche: *Most psychoses are characterized by a disordered* affect.

Effect is usually used as a noun to mean:

(1) End result or outcome: *What* effect *did the new employee have on our budget?*

(2) Influence or operative force: *The new regulations go into* effect *today.*

(3) Something that belongs to a person: *She lost her household* effects.

Used as a verb, **effect** means means to cause, produce, accomplish, bring about, or execute:

> *Will their efforts* effect *a change in the relationship?*
> *The committee hopes to* effect *a compromise between the two proposals.*

Because of the similar (but not synonymous) verb meanings of the two words, you may occasionally run into a sentence in which either verb may be used and make sense. In that case, the correct choice depends entirely on the intended meaning of the sentence:

> *He wants to* effect *(execute) a law on overtime pay.*
> *He wants to* affect *(act on or alter) a law on overtime pay.*

AFFECT/IMPACT: **Impact** as a verb meaning to pack firmly together is accepted usage. **Impact** as a verb meaning to affect is colloquial and disapproved by 95% of the experts. If you mean that something **affected** you, why not just say that it **affected** you (although that's pretty vague in itself!) As a noun, **impact** means violent contact or a shocking effect. Is that really what you mean?

AGNOSTIC/ATHEIST: An **agnostic** does not deny the existence of God, just claims that no one can know. An **atheist** denies God's existence entirely.

AGO/SINCE: **Ago** implies present to past and is always used following the noun: *It was five years* **ago** *that I was married.* (Better yet, *I was married five years* **ago.**) **Since** implies past to present. *It has been five years* **since** *I was married.* These words should never be used together.

AISLE/ISLE: An **aisle** is what the bride walks down (although that, too, is erroneous; she really walks down the nave). **Isle** is synonymous for island.

ALIBI/EXCUSE: An **alibi** is a <u>legal</u> excuse, a plea of being elsewhere when the offense was committed. An **excuse** is the apology or defense that the rest of us use.

7.8

ALIEN/ALIENIST/ALIENATE: All three of these terms imply difference or opposition. An **alien** is someone born in, or belonging to, another country (or world). It's also applied to someone excluded in some way (an outsider) and strange or unfamiliar matters. **Alien** also means repugnant (**alien** *to his religion*). An **alienist** is a psychiatrist, especially one who gives court testimony on questions of sanity. **Alienate** is a verb meaning to estrange, turn away, cause a transference of affection (or property).

ALLOW: See Acknowledge.

ALLUDE/ELUDE: **Allude** means to refer to in a casual way; **elude** means to evade. *My date* **alluded** *to monogamy as outdated, and he* **eluded** *it quite well.*

ALMOST: See Most.

ALREADY/ALL READY: **Already** is an adverb meaning previously or by this time. **All ready** is usually an adjective phrase meaning completely prepared.

ALTERNATE/ALTERNATIVE: Alternate can mean to go back and forth from one to another or to change at intervals:

>*Sue* alternated *between my house and hers.*
>*Jane was hired as an* alternate *to work on* alternate *days.*

Alternative indicates a choice among two or more possibilities, but it implies a certain imperativeness that *choice* does not: *She had only two* alternatives.

ALTHOUGH/THOUGH: These words both mean even *regardless, in spite of the fact that*, and may be used interchangeably in most instances. **Although** is more commonly used at the beginning of a sentence. **Though** is more commonly used in linking words and phrases (*sadder* though *wiser*) and is preferred at the end of a statement: *She looked good to me* though.

ALTOGETHER/ALL TOGETHER: All together is usually used as an adjective phrase meaning in one group: *We were* all together *last week.* **Altogether** is an adverb meaning entirely, completely, utterly: *The instructions were* altogether *too easy.*

AMONG: See Between.

AMOUNT/NUMBER: **Amount** refers to quantity and is taken as a whole; it relates to *less*. **Number** refers to individual units that can be counted separately; it relates to *fewer*. *We have* **fewer** *calories and* **less** *taste*. The exceptions are time, measurement, and money. You can have less than $5, even though *fewer* dollars and *less* money are technically correct. See Fewer/Less.

ANXIOUS/EAGER: If you're **anxious**, you're worried— filled with anxiety, agony. If you're **eager**, you're looking forward to the event with cheerful expectation.

ANYBODY/ANY BODY: **Anybody,** in the sense of any person, should not be written as two words. It's the same as *anyone*. **Any body** means any corpse or any human form or any group. The same rule holds true for *everybody, nobody, somebody,* for the same reason. In the sense of a live person, they are best written as one word.

ANYMORE/ANY MORE: Even though **anymore** meaning *now* or *hereafter* or *further* has been around for more than 75 years, 91% of the experts still frown on it. If you do use it, reserve it for statements with a negative connotation:

> *The movies are no good* **anymore.**
> *Television is hardly worth watching* **anymore.**

Any more means additional: *Do you have* **any more** *candy?*

ANYPLACE/ANY PLACE: **Anyplace** as one word is now accepted to mean anywhere, but **any place** might mean any particular place. The same is true of *everyplace* and *someplace*. *She traveled* **everyplace** *on her vacation* is not nearly as truthful as *She traveled* **every place.**

APPEAR/SEEM: **Appear** really means to come forth, be visible: *He* **appeared** *in a dream.* **Seem** means to appear to be (something): *She* **seems** *happy.*

APPRECIATE/UNDERSTAND/VALUE: **Understand** means simply to grasp the concept. **Appreciate** means to understand <u>and</u> recognize the worth of. **Value** is to rate highly because of worth.

AS: See Like.

ATHEIST: See Agnostic.

AUTHOR/WRITE: **Author** is a noun. **Write** is a verb. When two people write a book together, they *cowrite* it to become *coauthors.*

AVENGE/REVENGE: To **avenge** is to punish for wrongs or oppression (vengeance). To **revenge** means to punish as a retaliation, usually for a personal affront (to get **revenge**).

AVERAGE/MEAN/MEDIAN/MODE: **Average** and **mean** are synonyms for the figure derived by totaling a group of numbers and dividing by the number of items. The **median** is the point in the series with an equal number of items above and below it. The **mode** is the number that most often appears.

If five employees receive hourly pay of $12, $10, $9, $5, and $5, the *average* (or *mean*) of their salaries is $8.20, the *median* is $9, and the *mode* is $5.

AWHILE/A WHILE: **A while** is an article and a noun meaning a period of time. Use it with the prepositions *for* or *in.* It is always two words: *Stay for* **a while.** **Awhile** is an adverb meaning for a short period of time. It is never used with a preposition, since *for* is already included in its meaning, and it's written as one word: *Stay* **awhile.**

BAD/BADLY: **Bad** is normally an adjective, modifying a person, place, thing, act, or quality. **Badly** is normally an adverb, modifying a verb, adjective, or adverb. The problem comes when we use linking verbs like *feel, smell, taste, is, are, sound, look*, etc. If you want to say that you're unhappy about something, use **bad** (or good): *I feel* **bad** *(good) about that.* If you mean that your health is impaired, use **bad:** *I feel* **bad** *today.* If you mean that you've lost your sense of touch, use **badly:** *I feel* **badly** *(poorly) now that my fingers are frozen.* See good/well.

BESIDE/BESIDES: **Beside** means at the side of or near, in comparison with, or other than:

> *I stood* beside *my spouse.*
> **Beside** *yours, mine seems inappropriate.*
> **Beside** *you, who else is qualified?*

Besides means in addition to: *He ordered three hamburgers* **besides** *his pizza!*

BEST/BETTER: **Better** is the comparative degree; it's used to compare two items. **Best** is the superlative degree; it's used to compare more than three.

AMONG (more than two)

BETWEEN (two only)

BETWEEN/AMONG: **Between** ("by twain") has two in mind; **among** has several. However, **between** also connotes an intimate sharing among all concerned, each to each, one to one, so "between you and me and the gatepost" is an acceptable phrase. **Between** also indicates geographical placement: **between** *Atlanta and Birmingham.* Both are prepositions and take an object (**among** *the four of us,* **between** *you and me*).

BRING/TAKE: You **bring** something <u>toward</u> you, or someone else **brings** it toward you. You **take** something <u>away</u> from you.

BUST/BURST: **Burst** is the verb—present, past, and past participle—meaning to break. The only acceptable verb forms of **bust** are to make penniless, demote in rank, tame broncos, hit, and arrest. When these things happen, you're **busted**.

CAN/MAY: There is still a distinction between these words in formal English: **can** is used when indicating physical ability; **may** is used when indicating permission. The distinction is usually ignored in today's writing and speaking, especially in informal communication.

CAPITAL/CAPITOL: **Capital** is either wealth, or an upper case letter (think of the *a* in *tall*), or a city or town that is the seat of government. A **capitol** is a building in which a legislative body meets (think of the *o* in *dome*). The *U.S. Capitol* is always capitalized. *The* **capitol** *is always located in the* **capital.**

CHILDISH/CHILDLIKE: Both mean typical of a child. However, **childish** connotes foolishness (negative) when applied to an adult, and **childlike** connotes innocence (positive).

CITE/SITE/SIGHT: Cite is a verb meaning to refer to: *You must cite your source of information or receive a citation.* Site is a noun meaning place, scene, or point of something. Sight is what you see.

COHERE: See Adhere.

COLLABORATE/CORROBORATE: Collaborate (can you see *labor*?) means to work together. Corroborate is to confirm or strengthen (*to corroborate a story*).

COMPLACENT/COMPLAISANT: Although both come from the same Latin base, they have taken on different meanings. Complacent means self-satisfied, smug. Complaisant means willing to please, obliging.

COMPLEMENT/COMPLIMENT: Complement is both a noun and a verb, meaning the completion of something or to enhance something *(e=e)*. Compliment also functions as both a noun and a verb, but means to praise *(i=i)*. One article cannot praise another article. *The wine complements the food.*

COMPOSE: See Comprise.

COMPRISE/CONSTITUTE/CONTAIN/
COMPOSE: **Comprise** means include, contain, consist of: *The band* **comprises** (is composed of) *three instruments.* **Constitute** and **compose** mean to make up, form, be the elements of: *The instruments* **constitute** (or **compose**) *the band.* **Contain** means to hold or enclose.

COMPTROLLER/CONTROLLER: A **controller** is usually the chief accounting officer with responsibility for internal auditing in a business. A **comptroller** is the same person in a government setting.

CONNOTATION/DENOTATION: **Connotation** is the <u>implied</u> meaning of a word or phrase. **Denotation** is the <u>exact</u> or explicit meaning.

CONSCIENCE/CONSCIOUS: **Conscience** is a noun that denotes your reasoning ability (good v. bad). *You can have a clean* **conscience** *even if science wasn't your best subject.* Your **conscious** mind controls your actions. . .and your **conscience**.

CONSTITUTE: See Comprise.

CONTAIN: See Comprise.

CONTEMPTIBLE/CONTEMPTUOUS:
Contemptible means deserving of contempt; **contemptuous** means having contempt for.

CONTINUOUS/CONTINUAL: Continual means over and over again (intermittent). **Continuous** means without any interruption (incessant). If something is **continual**, it goes on and on, but stops in between, like rain. If something is **continuous**, it goes on and on without stopping, like life.

CONTROLLER: See Comptroller.

CONVINCE/PERSUADE: The original distinction— **convince** someone to <u>believe</u> something and **persuade** someone to <u>do</u> something—is gone. These words are now interchangeable.

CORROBORATE: See Collaborate.

COUNSEL/COUNCIL: These words are confusing because they can both be a noun meaning a group of people. **Counsel** refers to a lawyer or group of lawyers. It is both plural and singular. (The term "Legal Counsel" is always singular.) An easy way to remember this is to remember *counselor*. **Counsel** also means an exchanging of ideas or a discussion, as well as advice or guidance. As a verb, **counsel** means to give advice. So it can mean to advise, the advice itself, or the attorney giving the advice. **Council** is an administrative, legislative, or advisory body and can never be used as a verb.

> *The prisoners received* **counsel** *from their* **counsel**.
> *The town* **council** *met last week.*

CREDIBLE/CREDULOUS/CREDITABLE:
Credible means believable. **Credulous** means gullible, ready to believe. **Creditable** means deserving credit or praise. See Incredible/Incredulous.

CRITERION/CRITERIA/CRITERIONS:
Criterion is singular; **criteria** is the preferred plural; **criterions** is an acceptable plural.

CURRICULUM/CURRICULA/CURRICULAR:
The first is singular, the second is the preferred plural, the third is the adjective form.

DATA/DATUM: **Data** is now acceptable as both singular and plural.

DEDUCE: See Adduce.

DENOTATION: See Connotation.

DESERT/DESSERT: **Dessert** is *sweet stuff* to eat. A **desert** is only *sand.* The verb is always **desert**.

DESIROUS/DESIRABLE: **Desirous** means desiring, having or characterized by desire: *I am* **desirous** *of a chocolate sundae.* It's the sundae that's **desirable** (worth wanting or having).

DEVOTED: See Addicted.

DIE/DYE: When you **die**, you cease to live. The past tense is *died*; participle is *dying*. When you **dye**, you change the color of something. The past tense is *dyed*; participle is *dyeing*.

DISC/DISK: *Webster's New World Dictionary* gives some overlapping definitions, but prefers **disc** as a phonograph record and **disk** as a computer plate.

DISCREET/DISCRETE: **Discreet** means prudent in your own behavior (having *discretion*). **Discrete** means separate and distinct, not attached, unrelated: *She and I had very discrete ideas.*

DISINTERESTED/UNINTERESTED:
Disinterested means impartial, without private interests in an issue. **Uninterested** means bored.

DYE: See Die.

EACH: See Either.

EAGER: See Anxious.

EFFECT: See Affect.

EITHER/EACH: Originally, **either** meant one or the other, not both. **Each** meant more than one, but as individuals. That distinction is now gone and these words are interchangeable.

ELUDE: See Allude.

EMIGRATE/IMMIGRATE: **Immigrate** means to go/come into *(i=i)* a country. **Emigrate** means to leave *(e=e)* it.

ENORMITY/ENORMOUSNESS: **Enormity** means atrociousness, great wickedness: *the enormity of the crime.* **Enormousness** means huge: *the enormousness of the elephant.*

ENORMOUS: See Huge.

ENTHUSIASTIC/ENTHUSED: **Enthusiastic** is the proper adjective of the noun *enthusiasm.* **Enthused** is slang.

ETHICS/ETHNICS: **Ethics** is the singular and plural noun meaning a system of science or moral principles. The adjective form is *ethical*. **Ethics** are members of an **ethnic** group, especially a minority or nationality. The adjective **ethnic** designates groups with common cultural heritages that are neither Christian nor Jewish.

EVERYDAY/EVERY DAY: **Everyday** (one word) is an adjective and must modify a noun. **Every day** (two words) is an adverbial phrase that tells when something happens. *Her anger is an* everyday *occurrence; she seems to be angry* every day.

EVIDENCE: See Proof.

EXCEPTIONAL/EXCEPTIONABLE: Something **exceptional** is not ordinary or average; it's already an exception (a case to which a rule, principle, etc., does not apply). Something **exceptionable** is liable to exception, open to objection, likely to be treated differently.

EXCUSE: See Alibi.

FACET: See Phase.

FARTHER/FURTHER: **Farther** refers to a distance (far*ther* than far, and far*thest* of all). **Further** is an aspect of reasoning and should be used with intangible measurements, like time, degree, or quality: *I'm* **further** *along in my studies than you are.*

The verb is always **further:** *It will* **further** *your knowledge.*

FATEFUL/FATAL: Actually synonymous, although **fateful** is usually used with a feeling of prophecy and **fatal** retains with a feeling of death.

FAZE: See Phase.

FEET/FOOT: We commonly say, "*This is a six*-foot *board,*" despite the fact that *feet* is the plural of *foot,* and obviously six is more than one. This exception occurs because in Old English there was no distinctive plural, at least in the nominative and accusative cases. This lack of distinction has survived with nouns referring to measurement, and so we say, *two*-**hour** *show, ten*-**mile** *drive, six*-**foot** *board.* **Note the hyphens.** This use of the singular is proper only when it *precedes* the noun, and is always hyphenated because it becomes a compound adjective. If the noun comes first, the plural is used: a show *two* **hours** *long*, a drive *ten* **miles** *long*, or a board *six* **feet** *long.*

FEWER/LESS: **Fewer** indicates things that can be counted. **Less** indicates things that cannot be counted. Generally, use **fewer** before a plural noun, **less** before a singular noun: *I have* **fewer** *paychecks than you, but you have* **less** *money.* See Amount/Number.

FIRST/FORMER: **First** refers to the **first** of many, either in a series, in quality, or in time (**first** *in line,* **first** *in the hearts of his countrymen*). **Former** refers to the first of only two and relates to time (*a* **former** *spouse*).

FIT/FITTED: **Fitted** is preferred as the past tense of the verb *fit,* even though *fit* is not considered bad usage. The past participle is also **fitted.** *The dress* **fits** *today, as it* **fitted** *last year, and has* **fitted** *for many years.* *Befit* and *outfit* also take the extra syllable (befitted, outfitted).

FLAMMABLE/IMFLAMMABLE: Strange, but true, these words are interchangeable. **Flammable** makes more sense to me.

FOREWORD/FORWARD: A **foreword** is an introductory statement to a book, especially one written by someone other than the book's author. **Forward** means at, toward, or of the front.

FOOT: See Feet.

FORMALLY/FORMERLY: **Formally** means in a structured manner; **formerly** means previously. See First/Former.

FORMER: See First.

FORMERLY: See Formally.

FORTH/FOURTH: **Forth** means onward. **Fourth** is next after third.

FURTHER: See Additional, Farther.

GAIN: See Get.

GET/OBTAIN/SECURE/ACQUIRE/GAIN:
Careful users of the language use **get** for the broadest application—to come into possession of something in any manner. **Obtain** suggests the expenditure of effort or desire. **Procure** suggest active effort or contrivance. **Secure** implies that there was difficulty in obtaining and retaining something. **Acquire** implies a lengthy process in the acquisition. **Gain** always implies effort in the getting something advantageous or profitable. So you **get** *a present*, **obtain** *a raise*, **procure** *a settlement*, **secure** *a lasting peace*, **acquire** *an education*, and **gain** *notoriety*.

GOOD/WELL: Normally **good** is an adjective and modifies a noun or pronoun. **Well** is normally an adjective and describes a verb, adjective, or adverb. That sounds simple enough. However, we often get into trouble because of the exceptions: verbs that pertain to the senses *(look, taste, smell, feel, sound, appear, seem, become, grow, etc.)*. These verbs take an adjective because they're really used as linking verbs—verbs that describe existence and qualify the subject of a sentence—they tell how a subject <u>is</u>. They only take an adverb when they refer to an action of the body. For example:

> *The boy smelled* **good**. (He had a pleasant odor.)
> *The boy smelled* **well**. (His sense of smell was acute.)
> *She felt* **good** *about the car.* (She had a good feeling about it.)
> *She felt* **well** *about the car.* (She covered it carefully with her fingers.)

In accordance with that rule, a person in bad health feels *bad,* not *badly.* Logically then, a person in good health should feel **good**. Not so.

The discrepancy is that **well** is considered an adjective when referring to a person's health: *I'm feeling* **well**. The common phrase, *"feeling good,"* although widely used, is not yet considered grammatically correct. You have a **good** feeling, and you feel **good** about an idea, but you feel physically **well**. See Bad/Badly.

GOT/GOTTEN:
The use of **got** as a linking verb, meaning the same as "become," is acceptable in informal English. However, many people (including I) feel that the rather ugly monosyllable **got** is inappropriate (*I have* or *I have become* sounds much nicer).

Got in the sense of *must*, as in *I've* got *to go to the store,* should be avoided in favor if *I must* or *I need to*, especially in formal speech or writing.

Has/have gotten as the past participle of *get* is common in America (although not grammatically preferred by the experts), especially for the senses of receiving, becoming, or arriving. This usage has probably evolved from a desire to distinguish between possession, as in *I've got* a car, and acquisition, as in *I've* **gotten** *a car.*

Gotten is also used in the idiom *ill-gotten gains.*

HEALTHFUL/HEALTHY:
Healthful means giving health; **healthy** means already possessing health. *You eat* **healthful** *foods to stay* **healthy.**

HISTORIC/HISTORICAL: **Historic** means important or famous in history; **historical** means based on history. A novel is **historical**, but the signing of the Constitution was **historic.**

HUGE/ENORMOUS/IMMENSE/ TREMENDOUS: **Huge** suggest a very large thing (**huge** *building*). **Enormous** means exceeding what is normal (*an* **enormous** *nose*). **Immense** suggests size beyond the regular, but does not connote abnormality (**immense** *trees*). **Tremendous** implies that something inspires awe or amazement because of its size.

HUNG/HANGED: **Hanged** only applies to death by gallows. Only people are hanged; everything else is **hung**. With the passing of this type of corporal punishment, **hanged** is disappearing.

I: See Me.

IMMENSE: See Huge.

IMMIGRATE: See Emigrate.

IMPACT: See Affect.

IMPLY/INFER: **Imply** means to suggest, hint, express indirectly. **Infer** means to conclude from the evidence. *Speakers* **imply***; listeners* **infer.**

IMPRACTICABLE/IMPRACTICAL:
Impracticable means not capable of being carried out, unreasonably difficult. **Impractical** means not a wise thing to do. It is **impracticable** for a man to bear a child; it may be **impractical** for him to adopt one.

INCAPABLE: See Unable.

INCREDIBLE/INCREDULOUS: Something is **incredible** if it seems too unusual or improbable to be possible. The person who finds it improbable is **incredulous**—they are doubting, skeptical. *I was* **incredulous** *about the* **incredible** *amount of pizza she ate.* See Credible/Credulous.

INNUMERABLE/NUMEROUS: **Innumerable** means too many to be counted: *The sky contains* **innumerable** *stars.* **Numerous** means many or very many, but not uncountable: *The City Library has* **numerous** *books.*

INSURE/ENSURE/ASSURE: There is no longer a distinction between these words in the sense of *to make certain*, except for spelling. The preferred spelling on this side of the Atlantic is **insure**. Since **insure** is the only version acceptable in the financial sense, most people and many dictionaries just use it for everything.

IRONY/SARCASM: **Irony** is meant to be humorous; it's an expression in which the intended meaning of the words is the direct opposite of their usual sense. **Sarcasm** is from the Greek *sarkasmos*, "to tear flesh like dogs." It is a taunting, sneering, cutting, or caustic remark, intended to hurt the receiver. It may also be ironic, but doesn't have to be.

IRREGARDLESS/REGARDLESS: **Regardless** is always the correct word and it requires *of*. **Irregardless** is substandard.

ISLE: See Aisle.

ITERATE: See Reiterate.

ITS/IT'S: **Its** is the possessive case of the pronoun *it*. Just like the other possessives that end in *s—hers, his, ours, theirs, yours*—there is no apostrophe. **It's** is a contraction for *it is* or *it has*, and the apostrophe is used to indicate that a letter is missing: *it (i)s, it (ha)s.* See Pronouns, Chapter 8.

JUDICIAL/JUDICIOUS: Although **judicial** originally applied more in a legal sense and **judicious** more in a nonlegal sense, it's not hard to see why these words have become interchangeable.

LAY/LIE: **Lay** is a transitive verb and must have an object (lay *an egg*). If you can use the word *put*, you can use *lay.* **Lie** is intransitive and will never have an object *(I lie down).* Remember: You must **lay** something; you **lie** alone. See Set/ Sit. See Verbs, Chapter 8.

LEARN/TEACH: To **learn** is to come to know. To **teach** is to impart knowledge. A student **learns;** an instructor **teaches.**

LECTERN: See Podium.

LEND/LOAN: **Lend** is the more common verb. It is now permissible, however, to **loan** something). **Loan** is the noun, no matter what you borrow.

LESS: See Fewer.

LIABLE: See Likely.

LIE: See Lay.

LIGHTED: See Lit.

LIKE/AS: **Like** means having the same characteristics, similar, as if. **Like** can always be followed by just one word: *He looks* **like** *[a] peanut!* If that ending word is a pronoun, the pronoun must always be objective: *She looks* **like** *me.* (See Pronouns, Chapter 8.)

As means equally, for instance, to the same degree, in the same manner that, while. **As** is a conjunction, so it must have a clause: *Peaches taste good,* **as** *fresh fruit should.* If it's followed by a pronoun, the pronoun will be nominative: *She's* **as** *tall* **as** *I am.*

However, in common usage, **like** has replaced **as** in plurals where no verb follows:

> *My automatic elephant runs* like *a charm* (. . .as a charm runs).
> *The idea went over* like *a lead balloon* (. . .as a lead balloon does).
> *They worked* like *beavers* (. . .as beavers work).

Notice that **as** without a final verb would give these statements a meaning of substitution or disguise:

> *It works* as *a charm* (but it really isn't a charm).
> *It went over* as *a lead balloon* (disguised as a lead balloon).
> *They worked* as *beavers* (disguised as beavers).

Today's pattern of usage blurs these words, but a good writer will distinguish between them.

LIKE/SIMILAR TO: Use **like**.

LIKELY/LIABLE: **Likely** means apparently true, promising, such as will probably be satisfactory, and reasonable to be expected. **Liable** means legally bound, likely to have or suffer from, and something unpleasant or unwanted is reasonable to be expected. So, where they overlap, **likely** has a positive or neutral connotation; **liable** has a negative connotation.

LIT/LIGHTED: Both are acceptable as the past tense of the verb *light*, although **lit** is preferred. However, **lighted** is the more common adjective.

> *She has* lit *a cigarette.*
> *We saw the* lighted *hallway.*
> *He* lit *the* lighted *lamps.*

LOAN: See Lend.

LOATH/LOATHE: **Loath** is the adjective meaning unwilling, reluctant; it's usually followed by an infinitive. **Loathe** is the verb meaning to hate.

LOOSE/LOSE: **Lose** is a verb meaning to suffer the loss of. It's the opposite of *win*, and rhymes with *whose*. **Loose** is an adjective meaning not tightly fastened, or a verb meaning to free. It rhymes with *goose*. You can remember this by remembering the double *oo* in *tooth*—it looks *looser* than a single *o*.

LOOSEN/UNLOOSEN: Another of those strange words that are interchangeable. I prefer **loosen**.

LUXURIANT/LUXURIOUS: **Luxuriant** means growing in great abundance, lush *(a luxuriant head of hair.)* **Luxurious** means marked by luxury, rich, comfortable, sensous *(a luxurious suite).*

MALTREAT/MISTREAT: Now interchangeable.

ME/MYSELF/I: **Me** is always an object, **I** is always a subject. **Myself** is a reflexive and should never be used if **I** or **me** will work. See Pronouns, Chapter 8.

MEAN: See Average.

MEDIAN: See Average.

MEDIUM/MEDIA/MEDIUMS: In respect to communication, the channel of newspaper, radio, or television is traditionally a **medium** (singular). All three are **media** (plural). **Media**, however, is being used more and more often as a singular form with **mediums** as its plural.

MISTREAT: See Maltreat.

MODE: See Average.

MORAL/MORALE: **Moral** means ethical, virtuous, capable of making the distinction between right and wrong: *She is a* **moral** *person.* Of course she also has **morals** (principles). **Morale** is the state of your spirits: *The* **morale** *is high at our company.*

MOST/ALMOST: **Most** means greatest in amount, quantity, or degree; or in the greatest number of instances; or very. It's not a standard synonym for **almost**, which means very nearly but not completely.

NAUSEATED/NAUSEOUS: These words are not interchangeable. Something is **nauseous** (nauseating) if it <u>makes</u> you sick to your stomach. The victim of that sickness is **nauseated.**

NOISOME/NOISY: **Noisome** means harmful, offensive, smelly. *Although children are often* **noisome***, they are more often* **noisy.**

NUMBER: See Amount.

NUMEROUS: See Innumerable.

OBLIVIOUS/UNCONSCIOUS: If you are **oblivious** to (or of) something, you're forgetful or unmindful about it. If you're **unconscious** of it, you are totally unaware.

OBTAIN: See Get.

ON/UPON: Use **on**. Save **upon** for fairy tales.

PAIR/PAIRS: **Pair** is singular; **pairs** is plural.

PARTIALLY/PARTLY/PARTIALITY: **Partially** means being or affecting only a part: *The girly was **partially** paralyzed.* **Partly** means not fully or completely: *The house was **partly** complete.* **Partiality** is a particular fondness, liking, or prejudice for someone or something: *Her **partiality** showed during the elections.*

PENALIZE/SANCTION: **Sanction** now has two meanings: to approve and to **penalize!** I prefer **sanction** for approve, bless, sanctify, permit; **penalize** for prohibit, impose a penalty on.

PEOPLE: See Persons.

PER: See A.

PERSONAL/PERSONNEL: **Personal** is an adjective signifying individuality. **Personnel** is a noun meaning persons employed. *One* **n** *means one person; two* **n**'*s means more than one.* **Personnel** can sometimes be singular, sometimes plural. See Plurals, Chapter 8.

PERSONS/PEOPLE: It's always better to refer to a specific number of humans as **persons**. **People** is nebulous, and best not used with words of number. Use **people** with nonspecific modifiers like *many, few, some, hundreds.* **People** also refers to the members of a race or nation as a whole.

PHASE/FAZE/FACET: **Faze** is a verb meaning to disturb or daunt. **Phase** is a noun meaning a stage in a familiar cycle or development (not an aspect or a part). **Facet** means little face, and applies to any of the faces of a many-sided thing, like on a diamond. It does not mean *part* either.

PODIUM/LECTERN: A **podium** is a platform to stand on, like a dais or stage or riser (although technically a podium is smaller). A **lectern** is a stand to put notes on and stand behind. They are not interchangeable.

PRECEDE/PROCEED: **Proceed** means to go or move forward, especially after an interruption: *You may* proceed. **Precede** means to go before: *You may* precede *me.* Remember that the correct spellings of the participles are **proceeding** and **preceding.**

PRECIPITOUS/PRECIPITATE: The verb **precipitate** has many meanings, among them to fall steeply and to condense water vapor and cause it to fall to the ground. When rain falls, it **precipitates** and is *precipitation.* When a mountain is steep or sheer, it is **precipitous.** Weather can't be **precipitous.**

PREMIER/PREMIERE: A **premier** is the first minister of state. A **premiere** is the first performance of a show.

PREVENTIVE/PREVENTATIVE: **Preventative** is a needless variant. Use **preventive.**

PRINCIPAL/PRINCIPLE: **Principal** is a chief, often the head of a school. Remember that a *principal* is your **pal.** It might also be the money you have invested in something (**principal** *plus interest*). **Principle** is always a noun; it is a standard of conduct, an essential element, or a rule.

PROCURE: See Get.

PRONE/SUPINE: **Prone** means lying flat, with face down. The word for lying on your back is **supine.**

PROOF/EVIDENCE: **Evidence** is something that tends to prove. **Proof** results from enough evidence to establish a point beyond doubt.

PROVED/PROVEN: **Proved** is the preferred past participle (verb) of prove. **Proven** is usually used as the attributive adjective (one that comes ahead of the noun). *To become a* **proven** *technology, it must be* **proved.**

RAISE/REAR: Fifty years ago, the use of **raise** with children so infuriated Frank H. Vizetelly, then editor if the *Funk & Wagnalls* dictionaries, that he nearly exploded in his wrathful condemnation: "**Raised** should never be used in the sense of bringing human beings to maturity. Cattle are **raised**; human beings are *brought up* or, in an older phrase, **reared**." My faithful *Webster's New World Dictionary* lists many definitions of **rear**, among which is "to educate, nourish, etc. (*to* **rear** *children*)." This tells me that *WNWD* prefers to **rear** children. However, *Harper Dictionary of Contemporary Usage* says, "Today, **raise** in the sense of 'to **rear**' is perfectly good usage."

RAVEL/UNRAVEL: Strange, but true, these words are interchangeable except when **unravel** is used in the special sense of solving or clearing up a mystery or complication. I prefer **ravel** for the normal usage.

REAR: See Raise.

REAL/REALLY/VERY: **Real** is an adjective meaning actual: *It's a* **real** *diamond*. **Really** is the adverb meaning actually: *I am* **really** *angry*. If you mean **very**, say **very**: *It's* **very** *hot today*.

REGARD/REGARDS: You answer in **regard** to a question, and you have **regard** for your parents, and you **regard** taxes as a fact of life. All you do with **regards** is give them to Old Broadway; it means a greeting.

REGARDLESS: See Irregardless.

REGRETFULLY/REGRETTABLY: **Regretfully** describes the feeling of regret; **regrettably** expresses the fact that something is worthy of regret. *I* **regretfully** *decline your invitation.* **Regrettably** (It is regrettable that) *I can't attend.*

REITERATE/ITERATE: Close enough to be used interchangeably.

RESORT/RESOURCE: **Resource** applies to any thing, person, action, etc., to which you turn for aid in time of need. **Resort** is usually used as a final **resource**, qualified by last.

REVENGE: See Avenge.

REVERSAL/REVERSION: Although **reversal** originally meant a change to the oppisite state and **reversion** meant
a change to a former state, these words are now interchangeable. **Reversal** is more common in nonbiological and nonlegal
use.

SANCTION: See Penalize.

SARCASM: See Irony.

SECURE: See Get.

SEEM: See Appear.

SHALL: See Will.

SIMILAR TO: See Like.

SINCE: See Ago.

SIT/SET: **Set** is almost exclusively a transitive verb—conveying action from the subject to the predicate—so it must have an object. Like *lay,* **set** can be replaced with *put. You* **set** *a table,* **set** *a pencil down,* **set** *your hair.* **Sit** is an intransitive verb requiring no action and having no object. *You* **set** *something; you* **sit** *alone.* See Lay/Lie. See Verbs, Chapter 8.

SLOW/SLOWLY: Both are acceptable as adverbs to modify movement, as are *quick* and *quickly.*

SOMETIME/SOME TIME: As one word, **sometime** means at some indefinite or undefined time in the future: *I'll see you around* **sometime.** As two words, **some time** means just an indefinite or undefined period of time: *I waited* **some time** *before leaving. I haven't heard from her for* **some time.**

STANDING: See Ad hoc.

STATIONARY/STATIONERY: **Stationary** means in a fixed position. When something is *stationary,* it makes *nary* a move. **Stationery** is writing materials. When you use a p_e_n to writ_e_ on an env_e_lop_e,_ you use **station_e_ry.**

SUPINE: See Prone.

SUSPICIION/SUSPECT: **Suspicion** is the noun form of the verb **suspect.** When you **suspect** something, you have a **suspicion.**

TACK/TACT: A **tack** is a short nail. If you are referring to the ability to be diplomatic, the word you want is **tact.**

TAKE: See Bring.

TEACH: See Learn.

THAT/WHERE: To introduce adjective clauses, **where** is properly used only after nouns of place:

It was in the bar **where** *the teenagers congregated.*

In other contexts, **that** is appropriate:

I read **that** *Kay is writing a book.*

Both words are often used incorrectly:

Marriage is **where** *you put a ring on your finger before you put one through your partner's nose.*
(Better: *"Marriage" is putting a....*)

THAT/WHICH: **That** is a defining or restrictive pronoun. It introduces a restrictive or defining clause—one that supplies information essential to understanding of the noun and can't be omitted:

We need to pay the bills **that** *are due.*

Which is a nondefining or nonrestrictive pronoun and introduces a nonrestrictive clause—one that is set off by commas and can be left out of the sentence without any change of meaning to, or understanding of, the sentence:

The ice cream, **which** *is melting, is chocolate.*

If you feel the need for commas or pauses around the clause, use **which.** If not, use **that.** If in doubt, use **that.**

THAT/WHO: Technically, either is OK. The experts are now accepting **that** in place of **who**, but never *which* in place of **who**. *Which* applies only to nonhuman things. However, I believe that we, as human beings, deserve to be distinguished from the automobiles, trees, and bumblebees of the earth, and I still prefer to be a **who**, not a **that** (and I may not be the only person around you **who** feels that way).

THERE/THEIR/THEY'RE: **There** is an adverb meaning somewhere (*remember here*). **Their** is an adjective meaning belonging to them (*remember heir*). **They're** is a contraction of *they are* (the apostrophe denotes a missing letter).

THOUGH: See Although.

TILL/TIL/UNTIL: **Till** and **until** are synonomous. **Til** is not a word.

TO/TOO/TWO: **Two** is a number. **To** is a preposition showing direction. **Too** means *also*. The best way I know to remember this is to memorize the number and remember that *also* signifies more, so the word **too** has more *oo's* than the others.

TREMENDOUS: See Huge.

TRIUMPHAL/TRIUMPHANT: **Triumphant** describes the person who is celebrating a victory. **Triumphal** describes the commemoration of the victory. *A triumphant person threw a* **triumphal** *party.*

UNABLE/INCAPABLE: Both mean without the necessary power, capacity or ability, but **unable** usually refers to a temporary inability and **incapable** usually refers to a permanent or long-standing inablilty. **Unable** is always followed by *to*, **incapable** is followed by *of*.

UNCONSCIOUS: See Oblivious.

UNDERSTAND: See Appreciate.

UNINTERESTED: See Disinterested.

UNLOOSEN: See Loosen.

UNRAVEL: See Ravel.

UNTIL: See Till.

UPON: See On.

USE/UTILIZE: Stick with **use**. It came first and it's still stronger.

VALUE: See Appreciate.

VERY: See Real.

WHERE: See That.

WHICH: See That.

WHO: See That.

WHO/WHOM: See Page 8.8.

WHOSE/WHO'S: **Whose** is the possessive form of *who*. **Who's** is a contraction of *who is*.

WILL/SHALL: Use **will** unless you are showing strong determination in the third person: *They* **shall** *not pass this way!*

WRITE: See Author.

WORSE/WORST: **Worse** is the comparative degree; it's used to compare two items. **Worst** is the superlative degree; it's used to compare more than two. See Comparatives, Chapter 8.

YOUR/YOU'RE: **Your** is the possessive form of you. **You're** is the contraction of *you are.*

CHOOSE YOUR WORDS WISELY

CHAPTER 8: OTHER THINGS THAT CAUSE US PROBLEMS

VERB TENSES

One special problem group is verb tenses. Here's a list of some of the tenses we have trouble with and their preferred conjugations:

Principle Parts of Frequently Used Irregular Verbs

PRESENT TENSE	PAST TENSE	PAST PARTICIPLE
arise	arose	(have) arisen
be	was	(have) been
begin	began	(have) begun
bid (make an offer)	bid	(have) bidden
bite	bit	(have) bitten
blow	blew	(have) blown
break	broke	(have) broken
bring	brought	(have) brought
catch	caught	(have) caught
choose	chose	(have) chosen
come	came	(have) come
die (pass away)	died	(have) died
dig	dug	(have) dug
dive	dived	(have) dived
do	did	(have) done
draw	drew	(have) drawn
drink	drank	(have) drunk
drive	drove	(have) driven
dye (color)	dyed	(have) dyed
eat	ate	(have) eaten

fall	fell	(have) fallen
fight	fought	(have) fought
fit (in size)	fitted	(have) fitted
fly	flew	(have) flown
flee	fled	(have) fled
forget	forgot	(have) forgotten
freeze	froze	(have) frozen
get	got	(have) got, gotten
give	gave	(have) given
go	went	(have) gone
grind	ground	(have) ground
grow	grew	(have) grown
hang (a person)	hanged	(have, was) hanged
hang (draperies)	hung	(have, were) hung
hide	hid	(have) hidden
know	knew	(have) known
lay (an egg)	laid	(have) laid
lead	led	(have) led
leave	left	(have) left
lend	lent	(have) lent
lie (down)	lay	(have) lain
lie (fib)	lied	(have) lied
light	lit	(have) lit
pay	paid	(have) paid
plead	pleaded	(have) plead
ride	rode	(have) ridden
rise	rose	(have) risen
run	ran	(have) run
say	said	(have) said
see	saw	(have) seen
set	set	(have) set
shake	shook	(have) shaken
shine (glow)	shone	(have) shone
shine (polish)	shined	(have) shined
shrink	shrank	(have) shrunk
sing	sang	(have) sung
sink	sank	(have) sunk
sit	sat	(have) sat
speak	spoke	(have) spoken
spring	sprang	(have) sprung
steal	stole	(have) stolen
swear	swore	(have) sworn
swim	swam	(have) swum
swing	swung	(have) swung
take	took	(have) taken
tear	tore	(have) torn
throw	threw	(have) thrown
wake	woke	(have) waked
wear	wore	(have) worn

SUBJECT/VERB AGREEMENT

Verbs are the most important words in our language, and the most difficult for some people. We all know that verbs show the action in a sentence, like *skiing*. Verbs like *am, is, are,* and *become* are linking verbs—they link the subject with another word that identifies or describes it, like *being*.

One of the first rules we learned in Miss Boring's grammar class was that a verb must agree with its subject in number and person. The number of the subject determines the number of the verb. That sounds simple enough but, unfortunately, this rule is not always easy to follow.

Here are a few rules to help you select the correct verb:

(1) A compound subject joined by ***and*** almost always takes a plural verb.

(2) Singular subjects joined by ***or*** or ***nor*** take a singular verb.

(3) For singular and plural subjects joined by ***or*** or ***nor***, select the verb that agrees with the nearest subject.

(4) An intervening phrase coming between the subject and the verb should not be misconstrued as the subject and does not change the number of the subject: ***Freddie Fudpucker, as well as about 20 police officers,*** *sped down Highway 10.*

(5) These words take singular verbs:

each	anyone	no one	company
either	someone	everybody	group
neither	everyone	somebody	many a
one	anybody	somebody	more than one

These take plural verbs:

several	both	couple
few	many	

These take singular or plural verbs based on the noun they precede:

some	none
any	most

(6) Collective nouns, such as *family* and *committee* are usually singular. If the collective noun refers to the group as a whole or the idea of oneness predominates (which is more often true), use a singular verb: ***Each committee has to supervise its own affairs.***

COMPARATIVES

Another problem group is comparatives—modifiers (adjectives or adverbs) that can change degrees of intensity. Almost every modifier can be compared except ones that are already total (see Absolutes, below).

The comparative degrees are *positive* (*pretty*), *comparative* (*prettier*), and *superlative* (*prettiest*). And the basic rule is elementary. If there's only one, use the positive degree (*tall*). If you're comparing two of something, use the comparative degree—add **er** (*taller*). If you're comparing more than two, use the superlative degree—add **est** (*tallest*).

Of course there are some modifiers that don't change by adding *er* and *est*, but take the words **more** and **most**, **less** and **least** to signify comparison: *beautiful* (positive), *more beautiful* (comparative), *most beautiful* (superlative). Most adverbs compare this way.

Generally, words of one and two syllables, like *tall* or *pretty*, compare normally, with *er* and *est*. Words of three or more syllables, like *beau-ti-ful*, usually require **more** and **most**. This definitely is not a hard-and-fast rule, but will serve you well in most instances. Just remember to never mix styles; don't use phrases like *more happier, least best,* or *most tallest.*

The only comparable words I know that don't have all three degrees of comparison are *mere* and *further.* We speak of a *mere* detail, which is the positive degree, and a *merest* detail, which is the superlative degree, but never of a *merer* detail, which would be the comparative degree. There are comparative and superlative degrees for *further (further, furthest)*, but no positive (*fur?*).

Of course you know that there are a few irregular adjectives and adverbs that change in form as they are compared, like *good, better, best*; and *bad, worse, worst.* These just have to be memorized.

There's also one class of words that can't be compared at all because the words are already ultimate. These are called **absolutes**. Some examples are *perfect, unique, equal, final, first, last, fatal, total, unanimous, surrounded, pregnant, dead. Perfect* is just that—perfect. *Unique* means being without an equal, so something can't be *more* unique, *less* unique, or even *rather* unique. You can't be *partially* pregnant, just as you can't dig *half a hole*. And *dead* is the most absolute of all absolutes!

I'm dead tired.

PERSONAL PRONOUNS

Another problem group is personal pronouns, especially compounds. We have little problem choosing singular subject or object pronouns, but compounds seem to throw us. I think there's an easier, faster, safer way to conquer this problem than our high-school way of deleting one of the pronouns.

Personal pronouns fall into four cases:

Nominative (subject/head): *I, she, he, they, we, you, it, who*

Objective (object of verb or preposition/feet): *me, her, him, them, us, you, it, whom*

Possessive (ownership/adjective): *mine, hers, his, theirs, ours, yours, its, whose*

Reflexive (referring back): *myself, herself, himself, themselves, ourselves, yourself, itself*

These pronouns are somewhat snobbish—they never mingle or change categories. Therefore, if you need a subject, you'll always use one of the subject pronouns. If you need a compound subject, you'll always use two subject pronouns, never one subject and one object or reflexive. If you mentally substitute one plural pronoun—either *us* or *we*—for the compound, it all becomes clear. For instance:

He and she and I (we) had a good time watching the submarine races.

In my nightmare, Robert Redford asked her and me and all of them (us) for a date on the same night.

This is just between you and me (us).

He and she (we/they) wanted to see you and me (us).

The team consists of him, you, and me (us).

*He and I (**we**) got some ideas from the manager.*

*Jack and Jill and I and they and you (**we**) are the ones who (**we**) are responsible.*

If **we** works, all your compound pronouns must come from the subject category. If **us** works, all your compound pronouns must come from the object category. You'll never find a subject pronoun in the predicate, or an object pronoun in the subject. Choose the plural pronoun that works and choose your singular pronouns from the same category. And remember, the pronouns never change categories or join with another category word.

And it doesn't have to be a compound pronoun for the system to work. Substituting **we** or **us** works even with single choices:

*The meeting was between the president and him (**us**).*

*The manager asked Mary and me (**us**) to lead the meeting.*

*Since Joe is such a good speaker, the company asked him and Kay (**us**) to speak.*

*Both Ann and she (**we/they**) were promoted.*

*Will Jane or she (**we/they**) be there tonight?*

*She asked me (**us**) to make the call.*

*She asked that I (**we**) make the call.*

Who/Whom

Remember that **who** and **whom** are part of the above system. **Who** goes with *we/he* and **whom** goes with *us/him*. The difference between these two is not as critical as it used to be, but you should at least be aware of the difference, especially since the distinction is so simple to make.

*Kermit is the frog **who** Miss Piggy thinks is most handsome=Miss Piggy thinks **he** is most handsome.*

*He is the frog **whom** she hopes to kiss (presumably because he is so handsome)=She hopes to kiss **him**.*

*This is the person **whom** I asked to investigate=I asked **him** to investigate.*

*I can't see **who** is at the door=I can't see if **he** is at the door.*

It also works with interrogatives. Turn the question around, and if *he* fits, always use *who*. If *him* fits, always use *whom*.

***Who** do you think will be most boring?=Do you think **he** will be most boring?*

***Whom** did the caller ask for?=Did the caller ask for **him**?*

***Who** was the culprit?=Was **he** the culprit?*

By the way, it's always *whom* after a preposition.

The use of *that* for *who* is acceptable in informal English, but the use of *which* for *who* is not: *He is the nice man **who** (or **that**) said all grammarians are not short and fat.*

So: • *Use **who, whose,** and **whom** to refer only to people.*
   • *Use **which** to refer only to animals and things.*
   • *Use **that** to refer to any of the above.*

He/They

In formal grammar, **he** is still correct after a singular indefinite pronoun, like *anyone, everyone, anybody, either,* and *each,* unless of course you're talking specifically about females.

It's now acceptable, however, to use **they** in cases requiring a pronoun when gender is unknown: *If* anyone *calls, tell* them *I've gone to Siberia. Every* salesperson *can meet* their *quota this month.*

However, to use a singular antecedent with a definite gender and then use a plural reflexive pronoun is ludicrous. I heard someone say recently, *"Every woman now faces* their *own challenge."* And I heard on television: *"Any father would be glad to have you interested in* their *daughter"* Do you suppose those speakers weren't sure of the gender of *woman* and *father*? Avoid this type of error at all costs. If you mention a male or female, use a male or female pronoun.

Here are some additional pronoun guidelines:

• A **self** word—*myself, himself, herself, themselves,* etc.— should never be used as a subject or an object. They are used only to repeat or reflect on an already-stated subject: *I talked to* myself. Never use a construction like:

> *The argument was between* myself *and the manager.*
>
> *Kay and* myself *are pleased to welcome you.*
>
> *On behalf of the company and* myself, *we're glad you're a part of our team.*

• A personal pronoun following *that* will always be in the nominative case: *He asked that* I *leave early.*

• A personal pronoun following a linking verb (*is, are, were,* etc.) should always be in the subject case, with one exception: *It's* **me** is now generally accepted.

• The word to which a pronoun refers should always be clear to the reader. A pronoun may be used with grammatical correctness and still be confusing or misleading:

(1) *Billy told his brother that* **his** *money had been stolen.* The first **his** is clear enough, but the next **his** could refer to either Billy or brother.

To avoid ambiguity and awkward repetition, rewrite the sentence: *Billy said to his brother,* "**My** *money has been stolen.*"

(2) *She tried to avoid using slang,* **which** *greatly improved her communication.* **Which** has no clearly apparent antecedent, but refers broadly to the whole idea in the first clause.

Rewrite and supply a definite antecedent, substitute a noun for the pronoun, or just get rid of the pronoun: *She avoided using slang,* **a practice that** *greatly improved her communication.* **Her avoidance of slang** *greatly improved her communication.*

• A pronoun should not refer to a word that is merely implied and must be understood from the context:

(1) *My mother is a doctor.* **This** *is a profession I intend to follow.* The antecedent of **this** is **medicine,** which is implied in **doctor,** but is not actually stated. **Be specific:** *My mother is a doctor.* **Medicine** *is the profession I intend to follow.*

8.11

(2) *When she put a stick into the beehive, it flew out and stung her.* Be specific: *When she put a stick into the beehive, a bee flew out and stung her.*

• Avoid use of **you** and **your** unless you are speaking specifically about the reader. The pronoun **you** should never refer to an antecedent in the third person. Instead, use an impersonal word like **person**, or the pronouns **their** or **them**. (**One** is very old-fashioned, however.)

> *No matter what a person does,* **your** *mother still loves* **you.**

> *No matter what* one *does,* one's *mother still loves* **one.**

> **Change to:** *No matter what a person does* (you do), **his/her/their** (your) *mother still loves* **him/her/them** (you).

• A pronoun immediately preceding a gerund (a verb form used as a noun that translates into *action*) is always in the possessive: *I appreciate* **your** *arriving early* (your act). *My supervisor approved of* **my** *going home* (my act).

So after Nola told Philip that she didn't approve of her, he called their house and canceled his date with her. Then Jeff learned that she had left with Luke and he was very angry with him.

8.12

PREPOSITIONAL IDIOMS

Our next group of troublesome words is idiomatic prepositions. Usage requires that certain words be followed by certain prepositions. Using the wrong preposition can change the meaning of your sentence and prove that your grammar isn't up to par. Sometimes more than one word is correct, but often the choice depends on meaning. Here are the preferred choices for some common idioms:

Accede: To (a demand)

Accompanied: By (a person)
              With (a thing)

Account: For (a loss)
            To (a person)

Accused, Suspected: Of. A person may be charged *with* an offense, but must be accused *of* it.

Adjacent: To (something else)

Affinity: For (something or someone)

Agree: On—Reach an understanding. (*We agree on this.*)
          To—Accept another person's offer. (*I agree to your plan.*)
          With a *person*. (Two **items** in comparison also agree with each other.

All: Of (something)

> **Note:** Some experts argue against the use of *of* after *all*. If we rule out "*all of the pupils*" and say "*all the pupils*," the same logic should apply to "*all of them*." But it doesn't. Except with pronouns, the *of* following *all* may be omitted, but its use is well established and very acceptable.

Angry: At *or* About (something)
       With (someone)

Argue: About (something)
      With (someone)

As: Though (hypothetical situations). *Do not use "as* **if** *it were. . . ."*

Be sure: To (do something). *Never use "be sure* **and."**

(On) **Behalf of**:   As the agent of, in place of
(In) **Behalf of**:   For the benefit of

Capacity: Of (a container, room)
          To (understand, believe)
          For (work, play)

Center: Around: Physically impossible—don't use.
         Use *centers on, revolves around, concerns,* or *is about*

Circumstances: *In these circumstances* makes more sense than *under these circumstances,* since the stances are standing around (circum), not standing under

Compare: To (illustrate a likeness between two things)
With (examine two persons or things for likenesses and differences)

Comply: With (a rule)

Concur: In (a decision)
With (a person)

Confess: To (a crime)

Note: A prisoner can *confess a crime* or *confess to it.* But idiom, which often acts illogically, does not permit the same constructions to be used after *admit.* A prisoner can *admit a crime,* but can't *admit to it.*

Convenient: For (suitable for a purpose)
To (nearby, easily accessible)

Convince: Of (a fact)
That (something is true)

Correlation: Between *or* of (two things)

Correspond: To (match something, conform to it)
With (exchange letters)

Died: Of (cancer)

Differ: About *or* on (a particular issue)
 From (something else)
 With (a person)

Different: From (use in all instances unless clumsy)

Disappointed: In (a person)
 With (a tangible thing)
 At (something intangible)

Entrust: With (deliver in trust)
 To (commit something to someone)

Excerpt: Of (a paragraph—a part of the whole)
 From (an agreement—the whole)

Go: Into (don't confuse with go in *to see*)

Graduate: From (school)

Note: You can *graduate,*
and you can *graduate* **from,**
and the school can *graduate*
you, but you can't *graduate*
school.

Identical: To (match exactly)
 With (be consistent with)

8.16

Immune: To (a disease)
From (a regulation)

Independent: Of (free of the influence of another). *Never say "independent* from."*

Inside: Of (in less than). In other meanings, *of* is unnecessary

Intervene: Between (persons)
In (a dispute)

Key: To (an issue, a mystery, an answer, a door)
Of (a musical scale)

Liable: To (legally responsible to, **or** probable)
For (owing)

Part: From (leave)
Of (piece)

Payment: For (an article)
Of (a bill)

Persuade: To (do something)

Prefer: To (do something, **or** prefer one to another)

> **Note:** *Rather than* may be used instead of *to* only when *prefer* is followed by an infinitive: *I prefer to watch TV rather than to watch radio. Never use "prefer* over."*

Proficient: In (a skill)

Prohibit: From (doing something)

Quarter: To (a time)
Of (an amount)

Recognition: Of (services, appreciation)

Reconcile: To (circumstances)
With (a person or set of figures)

Retroactive: To (a certain date). *Never say "retroactive from."*

Should, Would: Have (done something). *Never use "should/ would of."*

Sick: With (a disease)
Of (something)

Similar, Dissimilar: To (another thing)

Speak, Talk: To (make a statement)
With (discuss)

Try: To (do something). *Never use "try and."*

Vexed: At (a thing)
      With (a person)

Wait: For (someone who is late)
     On (a customer)

BOX OR BOXEN?

We'll begin with *box*; the plural is *boxes*;
But the plural of *ox* is *oxen*, not *oxes*.

One fowl is a *goose*; two are called *geese*,
Yet the plural of *moose* should never be *meese*!

You may find a lone *mouse* or a whole nest of *mice*,
But the plural of *house* is *houses*, not *hice*!

If the plural of *man* is always *men*,
Why shouldn't the plural of *pan* be *pen*?

If I ask for your *foot* and you show me your *feet*,
And I give you a *boot*—would a pair be called *beet*?

If one is a *tooth*, and a whole set are *teeth*,
Why shouldn't the plural of *booth* be *beeth*?

One may be *that*, and three may be *those*,
Yet *cat* in the plural would never be *cose*;

We speak of a *brother*, and also of *brethren*,
But though we say *mother*, we never say *methren*!

The masculine pronouns are *he*, *his*, and *him*,
But imagine the feminine: *she*, *shis*, and *shim*!

So English plurals, I think you'll agree
Are the funniest words you ever did see!

PLURALS

We have no problem adding *s* to regular singular nouns. The problem arises when the nouns become irregular. To make sure you don't waste time checking the spelling of plural nouns when your time could be better spent, let's review the rules for forming irregular plurals:

(1) Form the plural of nouns ending in the "**f**" sound by adding *s*, or by deleting the *f* or *fe* and adding *ves* (*chiefs, knives, loaves*). With a few nouns, you have a choice of either ending (*elves, elfs; scarves, scarfs*).

(2) Form the plural of nouns ending in *y* preceded by a consonant or consonant sound by changing the *y* to *i* and adding *es* (*cities, secretaries*). **Note:** An exception to this rule is *standbys*.

Form the plurals of nouns ending in *y* preceded by a vowel by adding *s* (*valleys; plays*).

(3) Form the plural of most nouns ending in *s*, *x*, *z*, *h*, *ch*, or *sh* by adding *es* (*boxes, brushes*). **Note:** An exception to this rule is *quizzes*.

(4) Form the plural of nouns ending in *o* preceded by a vowel by adding *s* (*cameos, studios*).

Form the plural of nouns ending in *o* preceded by a consonant by adding *es* (*heroes, potatoes*). **Note:** This rule is not without exceptions. For example, to form the plural of music-related words, you simply add *s*: *pianos, solos*.

8.21

(5) To form the plural of most compound nouns and group words, add only *s* at the end, whether written as one word or several (*bookcases, cross-examinations, high schools*).

However, in some compounds, the more important part comes first, so you add the plural there (*poets laureate, sons-in-law, attorneys general, notaries public*).

Form the plural of compound nouns ending in *ful* by adding *s* at the end (*cupfuls, handfuls*).

(6) Form the plural of proper names by adding *s* or *es* (*Joneses, Smiths*). However, when the name is preceded by a title, you form the plural by adding *s* or *es* to either the name or the title, but not to both (*the two Miss* **Browns***; the three* **Drs. Black**).

(7) There is no definitive rule for forming the plurals of foreign words; some can be formed by adding *s* (*adieus*), some by adding *es* (*apparatuses*). Some retain their foreign plural form (*alumni, data*).

(8) The plural of a letter of the alphabet, or a word discussed as a word, is usually written with *'s*: *Mississippi has four* s's *and two* p's. *Study the three* R's.

But for words that stand for a concept, just add *s*: *Watch your* **dos** *and* **don'ts.**

(9) To make an acronym or a number plural, simply add *s* (*SNRs, CLSs, 9s*).

(10) When a substantive phrase—a phrase that serves as a noun—contains a possessive, form the plural by adding *s* to the second word (*master's degrees, debtor's prisons*).

These rules should help pluralize most of the words you encounter. There are, however, some special cases you must keep in mind:

• Some nouns (including all words ending in *ics* and *ies*) have the same form for both singular and plural (*mathematics, civics, morals, headquarters, series, species, aircraft, offspring, deer, moose, sheep*).

• Through usage, many Latin words that originally had both a singular and a plural have come into common usage in their plural form as both singular and plural: *data* (datum), *strata* (stratum), *graffiti* (graffito), *agenda* (agendum), *media* (medium), *trivia* (trivium).

• Some nouns are almost never used in the singular form (*barracks, goods, means, odds, trousers, pants*).

• Nouns surviving from the Old English form their plurals irregularly (*foot, feet; goose, geese; man, men; mouse, mice; tooth, teeth*).

• Most abstract nouns have no plurals (*purity, innocence, sagacity, patience*).

• Some nouns have two plurals, with different spellings and different meanings:

> ***geniuses***=people of genius, ***genii***=imaginary spirits
> ***indexes***=table of contents, ***indices***=signs in algebra

• The word ***fish*** depends on species. If you're talking about only one species of fish, the plural is ***fish***. If, however, you're talking about more than one species together, the plural is ***fishes***. Names of shellfish commonly use the general rule for plural formation (***crabs, lobsters, scallops***). ***Shrimp*** is singular and plural.

• Some words have one form that indicates both one and many. How the word is used in a sentence determines whether it's singular or plural (***beloved, educated***).

- These words are singular:

each	anyone	no one	company
either	someone	everybody	group
neither	everyone	every one	many a
one	anybody	somebody	more than one

These are plural:

several	both	couple
few	many	

These may be singular or plural, based on the noun they precede:

some	none
any	most

- Collective nouns such as *family* and *committee* are usually singular. If the collective nouns refers to the group as a whole or the idea of oneness predominates (which is more often true) use a singular verb: *Each committee has to supervise its own affairs.*

- If a compound modifier consisting of a plural number and a unit of measure is written before a noun, the unit of measure is singular: *a 25-person-per-elevator capacity, a 100-page-an-hour output, a six-foot bear.*

Note that if the number and the unit of measure were to come after the noun, the unit of measure would be plural: *a capacity of 25 persons per elevator, an output of 100 pages an hour, a bear six feet tall.*

Possessives

Possessives are used to denote ownership, source, or origin. We learned a long time ago that, to form the possessive of singular and plural nouns not ending in _s_, you add an apostrophe and an _s_. As for the rest, you merely add an apostrophe. In modern usage, this simple rule is no longer carved in cement. The following guidelines should help add to the confusion:

(1) If it has an _s_, don't add one; if it doesn't have an _s_, do add one. The apostrophe is mandatory and always follows the <u>base word</u>. ***Charles', Keats', Gomez's, Knox's, class' , soldiers', boys', Jesus', Degas', Does', Moses', Joneses'.***

(2) To indicate joint possession, put only the last name in the possessive form (**Jeff** *and* **Kay's** *house*). If the possession is not joint, however, put each person's name in the possessive form (**Jeff's** *and* **Kay's** *cars*).

(3) To show possession of hyphenated words, phrases, and names, put only the last word in the possessive form (**sister-in-law's** *husband,* **American-Daisy's** *publication*). If these words are plural (which you show on the main word), they still show possession on the last word (**sisters-in-law's** *husbands*).

(4) Use the apostrophe in forming the possessive of idiomatic expressions (*for* **appearance's** *sake, a* **moment's** *notice, at* **arm's** *length*).

(5) When words indicating the measurement of time or quantity are used as possessive adjectives, put them in the possessive case (*a* **year's** *work, a* **month's** *pay*). However, the trend today is to drop the apostrophe in the plural form *(two* **cents** *worth, two* **weeks** *vacation [a* **two-week** *vacation is even better]).*

(6) To form the possessive of expressions used with the word *else*, add an apostrophe and an *s* to the word *else* (*everybody* **else's** *opinion, anyone* **else's** *dream, someone* **else's** *fault*).

(7) There is a tendency to spell *one's self* as *oneself* in today's business world, and I think it will stick around, although it sounds too stuffy to me. The word *yourself* is better.

(8) Oddities often occur in the possessive form of company names. Remember that companies are single entities and become possessive just like other single entities. For instance, a company called *duPont and Associates* would own *duPont and Associates'* computer; *duPont and Assoc.* would own *duPont and Assoc.'s* computer. A company named *Ralph's,* however, is already possessive, so it will take no extra apostrophe. If *Ralph's* is attached to something, like *Ralph's Hotdogs,* the new company van will be ***Ralph's Hotdogs'*** van.

(9) Then there's the double genitive—*a friend of* **Kay's.** This is not really difficult when you think of it in the pronoun sense. You would never question *a friend of* **hers** or *a friend of* **mine.** Possessives all! In addition, there are rare instances in which the double genitive has a different meaning from the single genitive *(the picture of Mona Lisa* **vs.** *the picture of Mona* **Lisa***)*. But *'s* is only correct when *among* can be substituted for *of*.

(10) Plural words like *men, women,* and *children* do take *'s* when made possessive (**Women's** *Department,* **children's** *program,* **Men's** *Clothing*).

(11) The possessive form is not used in expressions where the possessive word is considered to be more descriptive than possessive (***United*** **States** *laws,* **company** *name,* **Georgia** *highways*).

(12) To form the possessives of nouns with irregular plural endings, first make the noun plural and then make it possessive: *the eclairs belonging to each lady* = *the* **ladies's** *eclairs;* the bicycles belonging to each child = *the* **children's** *bicycles.*

(13) The possessive of phrases is usually formed by adding *'s* to the last word in the phrase (***Kay duPont of*** **Atlanta's** ***book,*** ***Attila the Hun's attack***).

(14) For clarity's sake, be a little wordy sometimes and use *of* instead of possessives:

- With two possessives in a row: ***request* of *her brother's attorney***

- With a long, unclear possessive: ***policies* of *the Society for the Investigation of Criminal Abuse***

- With names that already contain a possessive: ***the quaintness* of *Martha's in the Vineyards***

- With a phrase that contains both a plural and a possessive: ***the outcomes* of *the mayors' elections***

(15) Holidays supposedly belonging to a special person or group seem to have no possessive pattern. These spellings are from *Chase's Annual Events: Special Days, Weeks, and Months*, Contemporary Books, Inc.:

Children's Day	Sadie Hawkins Day
Father's Day	Grandparents Day
St. Patrick's Day	Senior Citizens Day
Mothers Day	Special Olympics Day
Mother-In-Law Day	New Year's Day
Teacher's Day	Older Americans Month
United Nations Day	Valentine's Day
Veterans Day	President's Day
Secretaries Day	Family Day

ABBREVIATIONS

Remember the foreign language you encountered your first day on the job: "Did bx come COD attn Debra Jones, A/R Dept, or did mfg send it to hdqrs w/o inv for pmt?"

It may have taken you awhile to realize what all those unpronounceable and untranslatable abbreviations meant:

> *"Did that box come cash-on-delivery to the attention of Debra Jones in the Accounts Receivable Department, or did the manufacturing department send it to headquarters without the invoice for payment?"* (Hardly seems possible that they mean the same thing, does it?)

Abbreviations in business letters are often used to avoid repetition of long words and phrases or to save space and time or to reflect statistical data in a limited space, but they can be troublesome to the reader.

The occurrence of abbreviations in everyday business correspondence is directly related to the nature of the business. Some of you may never encounter an abbreviation. Some of you may use them every day. Some abbreviations depend on your own company's preference. If an abbreviation is important in your company's overall styling, by all means use it. But, normally, a letter filled with unnecessary abbreviations appears almost sloppy. As with all grammar questions, a good dictionary is your best source.

Let's look at some of the more common abbreviations as listed in *Webster's New World Dictionary, Third College Edition:*

AD = In the year of our Lord (from Latin, *Anno Domini)*

BC = Before Christ

aka = also known as

AM = after midnight (from Latin, *ante meridiem*—literally, before midday)

PM = premidnight (from Latin, *post meridiem*—literally, after midday)

> **Note:** If one minute before noon is 11:59 AM, and one minute after noon is 12:01 PM, is 12:00 considered AM or PM? Neither. It's *"noon."* Midnight is designated as *"midnight."* Incidentally, if you are writing of one minute later than 11:59 PM Saturday, it's midnight **Saturday**, not midnight **Sunday**.

> **Note:** Don't use *AM* or *PM* without specifying the hour; abbreviations are not used as substitutes for "morning" or "evening."

e.g. = for example (from Latin, *exempli gratia*). Used to introduce an example of a previous statement; not capped; set off by at least one comma; often italicized: *He wore everyday clothes to the party,* **e.g.,** *slacks and an old sweater.*

etc. = Plus others (from Latin, *etcetera*). The phrase is equivalent to "*and other things of the same kind*," so should not be used only if this meaning would be insufficient. Strictly applies to **things** rather than persons. Should be used only when it represents the last item of a list already given almost in full, or to immaterial things at the end of a quotation. Incorrect at the end of a list introduced by "*such as*," "*for example*," or a similar expression. Use of this word may suggest laziness. **Never use "and etc."**

FOB = free on board (seller pays freight or shipping charges to designated point)

G = gram(s)

HP = horsepower

i.e. = that is to say (from Latin, *id est*, "that is"). Used to repeat a thought that has already been said, but to repeat it differently or more clearly. Not capped; set off by at least one comma; often italicized: *He wore everyday clothes to the party,* **i.e.,** *he was inappropriately dressed.*

l = liter(s)

No = Number (Nos = numbers). Use only when referring to a list: *The book was* **No 1** *on the best seller list.* **NOT:** *What is the* **No** *of contestants on the swimming team?*

m = meter(s)

PhD = Philosophy Doctor

v = versus (in legal texts)
vs = versus (in general texts)

SOME GENERAL RULES:

(1) Spell out common courtesy titles unless they are used as a title preceding the name (***Dr. Helen Smith***).

(2) Always spell out cities, states and countries (except ***U.S.S.R***) within text. There are exceptions to this rule, but they apply to newspapers; federal agencies, policies, or programs; companies; armed forces.

(3) Always spell out street designations, days of the week, or names of months in text.

(4) Use an ampersand (&) only in company names, and only if the company does. ***Never use an ampersand in text.***

(5) Names of companies should be spelled out. Abbreviate ***Co., Inc., Ltd.,*** etc., only if the company does.

(6) Spell out areas of education, subjects and assignments:
Our assignment in biology *was to read* Chapter *6.*

(7) Omit periods and spaces in abbreviations of government or corporate names, and all other acronyms (*AFL-CIO, NASA, OSHA, SALT, NFL, OPEC, NBC, USAF, RCA, ZIP*).

(8) Write out educational or honorary degrees in text (*Bachelor of Science degree*).

(9) When using an abbreviation that may be unfamiliar or confusing to the reader, give the full form of the word or phrase first, followed by the abbreviation in parentheses. Thereafter, you may use only the abbreviation.

(10) Don't begin a sentence with an abbreviation, except for a courtesy title.

(11) Don't divide an abbreviation at the end of the line.

(12) Measures and weights may be abbreviated in figure + unit combinations but, if the numeral is written out, the unit must also be written out (*2 ft/sec,* or *two feet per second*).

(13) Limit all coined abbreviations to preferably three, but no more than four, letters. Abbreviations of five or more letters defeat the purpose. Use either the first letters of the word (*rec* for *receive*) or the letters that best represent the sound of the word (*intl* for *international*). If a word could have more than one ending, add the last letter of the ending (*recd* for *received* or *recr* for *receiver*). If two words are to be abbreviated, use a three-letter abbreviation for each word (*bal sht* for *balance sheet*). **These abbreviations are not considered contractions and do not need apostrophes.**

(14) Abbreviations are capitalized if the words represented are normally capitalized (*Fahrenheit, November*).

(15) When using **AM** or **PM**, all caps are preferred, without periods. If you use lowercase letters, do use periods (*a.m.*).

(16) Don't abbreviate in inside addresses of business letters, except for the accepted postal abbreviation of states.

(17) Omit spaces between the letters of abbreviations except a person's initials (*R. L. Stevenson, PO Box, U.S.S.R.*).

(19) Abbreviate as much as possible when addressing envelopes. Make sure you know the proper abbreviations of state, road, street, etc. **See Chapter 10.**

> *A man can have many virtues and abilities, but if he does not use language accurately and carefully, he can be a positive menace to a business enterprise.*
>
> *—Edwin A. Locke, Jr.*

WHEN IN DOUBT, DON'T CAP!

CAPITALIZATION

Capitals are used for two broad purposes: They mark a beginning, such as the beginning of a sentence, and they signal a particular person, place, thing, or group.

Capitalization is not an exact science. Sometimes a word should be capitalized, and other times the same word should be totally lowercased. Frequently a capital letter or a small letter would be <u>equally</u> correct. But there are some basic rules about capitalization that every writer should know.

(1) **Abbreviations** are capitalized if the words they represent are proper nouns or adjectives.

(2) The **first word of a sentence** or sentence fragment standing alone in parentheses is capitalized: *I will go. (No!)*

However, the first word of a parenthetical phrase or sentence occurring within another sentence is lowercased: *She studied under Dr. Brown (**he** wrote the text) at school.*

(3) The names of **schools and colleges** are capitalized, but *school* and *university* are lowercased when not part of a name:

>*I went to the **university** in Atlanta, but he went to Auburn **University**.*

The names of studies are not capitalized unless a particular course is indicated. School classes and grades are not capitalized.

(4) The first word of a **direct quotation** is capitalized if it begins a complete sentence.

However, a split quotation should be lowercased at the beginning of its continued segment: *"**The** Administration has denied the story," the paper reported," **and** the President feels the media are irresponsible."*

(5) Do not capitalize **indirect quotations:** *She said she was happy today.*

(6) Capitalize the names of **legislative, administrative,** and **deliberative bodies.** Capitalize *Legislature* and *Administration* when they stand alone and refer to a specific body.

(7) The word **President,** or any other word designating the President of any government, should always be capitalized.

(8) Capitalize all **titles or designations** preceding names, but lowercase titles following names or used instead of names: *James Brown, **president** of our bowling team, has been in the hospital. Presiding was **President** James Brown.*

Do not capitalize these titles if they are used alone or with a possessive pronoun or article: *Our **treasurer** is ill.*

When a common noun precedes a name but is separated from it by a comma, the noun does not have the force of a title and is not capitalized: *Let's welcome our former **senator**, Mary Strange.*

8.38

(9) The first word of a **direct question** within a sentence, or a series of questions within a sentence, may be capitalized: *The question is:* **Is** *man an ape?* **An** *angel?* **An** *artichoke?*

(10) The first word **following a colon** should be capitalized if it introduces a complete sentence or quote unless it merely explains or illustrates the point made in the first part of the sentence:

> *The answer is:* **You** *just don't know.*
> *It's easy to see why Billy's fat:* **he's** *always eating.*

The first word is also capitalized if the colon is preceded by a word such as *Note, Caution,* or *Reminder.*

Do not capitalize after a colon when the materials following the colon can't stand by itself as a sentence: *We need the following items:* **two** *chairs, one desk, three lamps.*

(11) The first word of **enumerations** that form complete sentences are capitalized: *The advantages of the inventories are: (1)* **The** *technique is economical. (2)* **The** *information is available.*

However, if the phrases don't form complete sentences, or are not preceded by a colon, don't capitalize: *The following sequence has proved effective: (1)* **demonstration,** *(2)* **practice,** *(3)* **questions.**

(12) The first words of **phrasal lists, enumerations,** and **out-lines** are capitalized:

> *Our areas are divided into the following segments:*
> *(1) Business, marketing, and management*
> *(2) Personal and public services*

> *We need to:*
> • *Get the warehouse cleared out*
>   *--Ask Brenda to help*
>   *Credit her account*
> • *Install the connector lines*
> • *Notify Ben Murphy of the due date*

>   *I. Production responsibilities*
>   *A. Cost estimates*
>   *B. Inventory appraisal*
>   *II. Marketing responsibilities*
>   *A. Needs analysis*
>   *B. Brochure design*

(13)   The words *Whereas* and *Resolved* are capitalized in minutes and legal documents. So is the second word of the declaration:

> *Whereas, Substantial benefits are to be derived from attending this workshop, it is hereby Resolved by the Executive Committee. . . .*

> *Resolved That each employee will. . . .*

(14)   Names of **awards** and prizes are capitalized: *I would love to win the Nobel Prize for Literature.*

(15)   Words designating **God** are capitalized (*God, Jehovah, Thee, Thou, Supreme Being*).

Also capitalized are those words relating to all **religions**, their heads, followers, sacred writings, idols, and holy days (*Virgin Mary, Book of Common Prayer, Holy Writ, Apostolic Delegate, Good Friday*).

(16) **Epithets** (words characterizing a person or thing) are capitalized: *Billy the Kid, Mack the Knife, the Board of Directors*.

(17) **Personifications** (names used instead of the actual name) are always capitalized. If you're talking about the President, you might say, "*the White House has announced.*"

(18) The **seasons** are never capitalized unless they are personified: *Gentle Spring has murdered Old Man Winter*.

(19) **Directional words** are capitalized when they refer to a specific geographical region, or when they are part of a street name (*out West, down South, up North, the Middle West, the West Coast, East Houston*), but are lowercased when they refer to a simple direction (*west of the Rockies, traveling east, the southern coast of Florida*).

Directional words are also usually capitalized when used as adjectives to designate the inhabitants of certain areas (*Southern accent, Western drawl, Northerners*).

8.41

Popular names of localities are also capitalized (*The Corn and Wheat Belts, the Gold Coast, the Loop, the Eastern Shore, City of Brotherly Love*).

(20) **Generic terms,** like *river, ocean, state, city, street,* are capitalized if they are part of the total name (*Lake Michigan, Pacific Ocean, Mississippi River*). However, if these names are preceded by the word *the*, the generic terms are lowercased because they refer to places in general (*the Mississippi and Missouri rivers, the lakes Michigan and Superior, the Ohio River valley*).

(21) Words like **mother** and **father** are not capitalized unless used as a proper name: *I wrote a letter to my mother. I talked to Father today.*

(22) The word **federal** is capitalized only when it is an essential element of a name or title, or when it identifies a specific government, agency, or organization: *The suit filed by the Federal Government finally ended up in federal court.*

Don't capitalize *state* when it's used in a general sense and does not follow a proper name (*the state of Georgia, federal and state governments.*

(23) The names of **political parties** and their followers (*Democrats, Republicans*) are capitalized. Capitalization of the word *party* is optional (*Democratic Party*).

(24) All **specific-designation adjectives** are capitalized: *My boss asked me to take this Special Delivery letter to the post office.*

(The words *post office* do not constitute a proper noun, so they are not capitalized. The proper name of the public agency that delivers the mail is **United States Postal Service**).

(25) The words **company, corporation,** and **club** are capitalized when they refer to your own organization, even when the full organization name is omitted. The words are not capitalized when they refer to someone else's company or club: *That holiday is contrary to Company policy, even though their company allows it.*

Of course these words are always capitalized when part of a title.

(26) The first letters of **monetary units** typed in full are capitalized. This includes monetary unit words typed on checks and in letters. The secondary part of a hyphenated numeral, however, is not capitalized: *Your check should be in the amount of Forty Dollars and Thirty-five Cents.*

(27) Nouns introducing **identification numbers** or **letters** are capitalized (*Order 123, Policy 456, Flight 789, Exhibit A*).

(28) Nouns followed by numbers or letters to designate **references** are capitalized (*Book II, Volume V, Page 1, Division 4*).

(29) Designations of **parts of books** are capitalized (*Table of Contents, Preface*).

(30) **Time zones** are capitalized when abbreviated (*EST*), lowercased when written out (*eastern standard time*).

(31) Capitalize the principal words in **titles** of books, magazines, articles, songs, etc. Do not capitalize the articles *a, an,* or *the,* or prepositions or conjunctions of two or three letters, unless they appear at the beginning of a title or follow a colon. Descriptive nouns following publication titles are lowercased (*The Wall Street Journal,* the *Oxford American Dictionary, Time* magazine*)*.

(32) Capitalize **hyphenated words** according to the way the parts would be written if they stood alone (*pro-German, Spanish-speaking, ex-President*).

(33) Capitalize nouns indicating **race, nationality,** ethnic group, language (*American, French, Black*).

NUMERALS

One of our language's trickiest questions is when to spell out numerals and when to use figures. Actually the answer often depends on the kind of document you're preparing. In extremely formal, legal, financial, or court-issued documents, all numbers—even years—might be spelled out. In statistical and tabulation writing, numbers are normally expressed in figures. Most business letters and other documents fall somewhere in between and use a combination. And some companies have their own set of rules to follow.

These guidelines relate only to numbers in sentences. It's elementary to review statistical or tabulation typing, since those are always done in figures. Remember, please, that these are only general rules and they may differ from the ones your company uses. The important thing to remember is that, whatever rule you follow, you should always follow it consistently.

EXPRESS IN WORDS:

(1) Numbers beginning a sentence.

(2) Numbers between one and ten.

(3) Round numbers (*two hundred*) and approximate numbers (*about thirty-five*).

(4) Even-dollar amounts (if figures are used, omit decimal point and zeroes).

(5) Numbers in formal writing, such as proclamations and invitations.

(6) Single fractions. Note that fractions used as nouns are not hyphenated (*two thirds of the cake*), but fractions used as adjectives are hyphenated (*two-thirds majority*).

(7) Ordinals (*first, hundredth*).

(8) Centuries (*twentieth century*).

(9) Measures and weights when the unit is spelled out (*six ounces*).

(10) Approximate time (*about six PM*), and always when *o'clock* is used (*six o'clock*).

(11) Age expressed in one unit (*twelve years old*).

EXPRESS IN FIGURES:

(1) Numbers of 11 and over.

(2) Percentage numbers (*25 percentage points, 0.5 percent*). Percent is acceptable either as *percent* or %, but don't mix units (*10%* **NOT** *ten %*).

(3) Monetary amounts in series. All figures in the series should contain the dollar sign, amount, decimal point, and four figures, even if the series includes an even or approximate amount, unless all amounts are even, in which case you should use only the main figures (*$6.50, $10.00, $12.81,* **OR** *$2, $6, $10, $26*).

(4) Amounts of less than a dollar (*10 cents* **OR** *10¢*).

(5) Numbers of policies, catalogs, contracts, pages.

(6) Numbers of streets, apartments, rooms, suites.

(7) Numbers of sizes, shares, degrees, scores, telephones.

(8) Fractions occurring in series. **When all fractions are not included on your keyboard, don't use any that may be.** If you're typing *1 1/2" x 1 1/8"*, and you have the fraction key for *1/2* on your typewriter but not the fraction key for *1/8,* don't use the *1/2* key. **Note that these units are typed with no hyphen.**

(9) Measures and weights with abbreviated units (*10 sq. ft., No. 4*).

(10) Numbers plus units in a series, even if the amounts are less than 11 or approximate. In all cases, the style for the higher number governs the series: *We need 5 chairs, 15 tables, 125 note pads.*

(11) Dimensions (*10 ft. x 12 ft.*). The signs for *feet ('),* *inches ("),* and *by (x)* may be used in all business writing.

(12) Exact time (*10:00, 10 AM*).

(13) Age in years, months, days: *He is 1 year, 6 months, 3 days old.*

EXPRESS IN WORDS AND FIGURES:

(1) Back-to-back numbers. When two numbers comprise one item or unit, the first should be expressed in words and the second in figures (*the two 4-drawer files*).

However, if the second number is much shorter, it may be expressed in words instead, with the first in numbers (*the 25 ten-drawer files*). **Note hyphens.**

(2) Numbers in succession: *By 1986, one hundred shares of stock will have been sold.*

(3) Numbers of 1 million and over (*$10 million* **OR** *10 million dollars*).

REMINDERS:

(1) Don't use **and** or commas between numerical units (*Twenty-five Thousand Four Hundred ~~and~~ Twenty-one Dollars*).

(2) Do use a hyphen in compound numbers under 100 (*twenty-six*).

(3) Don't use a decimal point plus the symbol ¢ or %, unless you mean a fraction of one cent or one percent (.45¢ is 45/100 of one cent; .35% is 35/100 of one percent).

(4) Don't follow fractions expressed in figures with **th, ths, of a,** or **of an:** *The size is 1/2 in. wide by 3/8~~ths~~ in. long. I need 3/4 ~~of a~~ yard of material.*

8.48

(5) Don't use a fraction with the word *percent* or the symbol %. Change the fraction to a decimal.

(6) Remember that when a fraction is joined to the number *one*, the following noun is plural. The verb, however, is singular: *The amount required is 1 3/8 inches. The distance was 1 1/2 miles.*

(7) Don't use *the*, *st*, or *rd* with dates followed by the year (*June ~~the 2nd~~, 1990*).

(8) Don't use both numerals and words for amounts, except in legal documents: *The amount due is Twenty-three Dollars ($23)*. Use numerals.

CHAPTER 9: PUNCTUATION

Punctuation is not really difficult if you understand its purpose. It's not for the *writer's* benefit, it's for the *reader's* benefit. Punctuation is used to express in writing what you can express face-to-face with modulation and body language.

You can easily tell if people are being facetious by their tone of voice. Picture someone at a party smiling broadly and saying, "I'm bored to tears. Can't we get out of here?" They're smiling for the hostess to see, but are they having a good time? No! How do you know? Because of their modulation. If I say to you, "Well, I'd like to go but, you know. . .," and shrug my shoulders, you <u>do</u> know.

You can express the same emotions through punctuation. Each mark has a specific purpose and they are seldom interchangeable. I've heard people say, "Oh, I used a semicolon because I wanted a stronger pause than just a comma." That reasoning won't work. "Well, I used a comma because I felt like the sentence needed emphasis." That reasoning won't work either. Each mark has a purpose. We wouldn't need them all if they didn't have jobs of their own.

KAY'S PUNCTUATION LIGHT

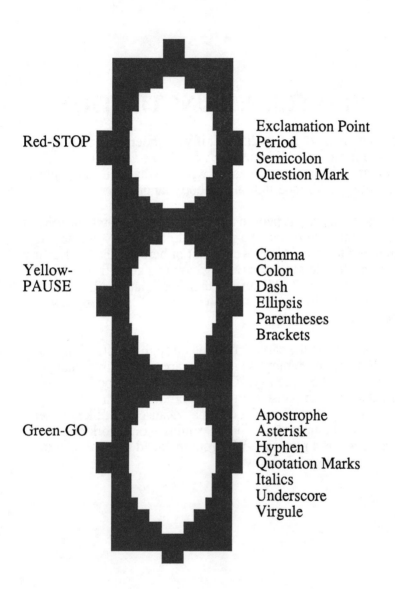

Red-STOP

Exclamation Point
Period
Semicolon
Question Mark

Yellow-
PAUSE

Comma
Colon
Dash
Ellipsis
Parentheses
Brackets

Green-GO

Apostrophe
Asterisk
Hyphen
Quotation Marks
Italics
Underscore
Virgule

I think the easiest way to remember the functions of punctuation marks is to divide them into groups, so I've developed a handy gadget called a punctuation light for this purpose.

Picture a traffic light. You're going down Main Street and the light is green, so you keep going. If the light is yellow, you slow down and look both ways. If the light is red, you know you must stop. We all follow the same rules. If we didn't, the result would be chaos—there would be bodies all over Main Street.

Punctuation signals work the same way. They tell our readers when to go, when to slow down, when to stop. Let's look at the punctuation light:

The **red lights**—the stop marks—are the period, exclamation point, semicolon, and question mark. All of these marks say, *"Stop, Reader. I've just finished a complete thought. Now I'm going on to another complete thought."*

You know, don't you, that the **question mark** shows that you're asking a question? The other three stop marks are interchangeable, but have different degrees of finality. The **exclamation point** shows emotion! The **period** shows fact. The **semicolon** also shows completion of a fact; however, it's followed by another complete, related fact. **The semicolon and the period are usually interchangeable.** Put simply, if you can't use a period, you can't use a semicolon (there are only two exceptions)!

The **yellow lights**—the pause marks—are the comma, colon, dash, ellipsis, parentheses, and brackets.

The comma says, *"Slow down, Reader. I have just stated a complete thought, and now I'm going to give you another closely related thought."*

9.3

The colon says, *"Slow down, Reader. I've just given you a complete sentence, and now I'm going to elucidate on that sentence: I'm about to name, or further explain, what I've just said."*

The dash says, *"Slow down, Reader. I've just stated a complete thought, and now I'm about to say the same thing in different words—I'm going to repeat myself. I may instead be interrupting my main thought to make a side statement, but please slow down and see what I'm doing."*

The ellipsis says, *"Slow down, Reader, and realize that I'm quoting someone else and have left out some of their words. I didn't think the words were important enough to to use here, but I want you to know I've left them out. I might instead be leaving out some of my own words at the end of a sentence so you can fill in the ending."*

The parentheses say, *"Slow down, Reader, and see that I'm enclosing some parenthetical material. It's not important enough to be part of the main sentence, so read what's here, but continue your main thought."*

The brackets say, *"Slow down, Reader, and see that either there are two parenthetical thoughts in this sentence or I'm commenting within someone else's quote."*

The **green lights**—the go marks—are the apostrophe, asterisk, hyphen, quotation marks (single and double), virgule, and underscore.

The apostrophe says, *"Don't slow down, Reader, but see that I have either left out a letter of the alphabet or I'm making something possessive."*

The asterisk says, *"Don't slow down, Reader, but, when you've finished this thought, go to the bottom of the page and see my footnote."*

The hyphen says, *"Don't slow down, Reader, but see that I am connecting multiple words into one. These words should now be considered either a single adjective or a single noun."*

The quotation marks say, *"Don't slow down, Reader, but see that I'm quoting something."*

The virgule says, *"Don't slow down, Reader, just realize that I am either representing the word **per** or separating alternatives."*

The underscore and italics say, *"Don't slow down, Reader; just realize that this word is either important, different, or a title of something."*

If you've learned to write a simple sentence (see Chapter 4), you should be able to use the proper punctuation no matter how complicated the sentence becomes. Your readers must be guided from the subject to the predicate, and using the punctuation light will help. If you want them to stop, use a red light. If you want them to slow down, use a yellow light. If you want them to keep going, use a green light.

The following rules outline the purpose of the punctuation marks in American writing (British is somewhat different), and also deal lightly with the exceptions.

EXCLAMATION POINT

An Exclamation Point Is Used To:

(1) End an emphatic or imperative phrase or sentence: *Mail it now!*

(2) Terminate an emphatic interjection: *Encore!*

Position With Quotation Marks:

(1) Inside quotation marks, if it belongs to quoted matter.

(2) Outside quotation marks, if it's not part of the quoted matter.

PERIOD

(1) To terminate:

   (a) A declarative or imperative sentence—one that does not ask a question and is not particularly emphatic or excited: *I ate the ice cream.*

   (b) Declarative sentence fragments, if they must be used: *Take a number.*

   (c) Polite requests, especially in business correspondence: *Will you send me a copy.*

   (d) Indirect questions: *She asked if you would be there.*

(2) Although periods to indicate abbreviations are vanishing, some still remain. See Abbreviations, Chapter 8.

   (a) Courtesy titles other than *Miss: Mr., Mrs., Ms., Dr.*

(b) Initials: *Z. A. Zebulan.* **One space between a person's initials.**

(c) Some geographical names: *U.S., U.S.S.R.* **No space between letters.**

(d) Some parts of corporate names: *Inc., Co., Ltd.*

(e) Latin words and phrases commonly used in text (*etc., i.e., e.g.*) and footnote references (*ibid., Op. cit.*). **No space between letters.**

(f) Measures of time and designation: *P. 20, 18 in., No. 2.* **Note spaces.**

(3) With some numerals:

(a) After Roman numerals in enumerations and out-lines, but not when used as part of a title:

RIGHT: ***I.** **Ice Cream***
            A.** **Chocolate
            B.** **Pistachio

WRONG: ***Freddie Fudpucker, III.***

(b) With Arabic numerals in enumerations whose numerals stand alone without parentheses:

We will discuss the following areas:
1. Love
2. Hate
3. Empathy

Position With Quotation Marks: Always inside quotation marks, no matter what the sentence structure.

SEMICOLON

(1) Precedes transitional expressions and conjunctive adverbs that introduce main clauses:

accordingly, besides, then, therefore, thus, consequently, furthermore, however, for example, in fact, for instance, that is, that is to say, namely, e.g., i.e.

Always use a comma after those introductory words: *I don't want to go; however, I will if you can find a date for me.*

(2) Separates members of a series when any one or all the series already has a comma:

The following members were present: **John January, President; Jane February, Vice President; June March, Secretary.**

(3) Links two or more independent clauses not joined by a conjunction to form a single compound sentence. The semicolon indicates omission of the conjunction: *Secretaries make better friends; they're the type.* It is equally correct, of course, to write each of those clauses as sentences, replacing the semicolon with a period. If a conjunction is inserted, the proper mark is a comma: *To err is human, and to forgive is saintly.*

An exception to this rule is worth noting here. A comma is preferable when the clauses are very short and alike in form, or when the tone of the sentence is easy and conversational:

> *Man proposes, God disposes.*
> *The gates swung apart, the bridge fell, the doors opened.*
> *I came, I saw, I conquered.*

(4) Separates contrasting <u>clauses</u> without a conjunction: *I came to conquer; to surrender would be unthinkable.* Use a comma to separate contrasting <u>phrases</u>: *He has changed only his style, not his ethics.*

(5) Separates coordinate elements joined by a coordinating conjunction but internally punctuated: *I love Jeff, Bob, Tom, Charles, and Larry; but George, Henry, and Leon are very special.*

Position With Quotation Marks: Always outside.

QUESTION MARK

Everyone knows to use a question mark to indicate a direct question in writing. But there are a few additional points to remember about the question mark.

A Question Mark Is Also Used To:

(1) Punctuate each element of an interrogative series that is neither numbered nor lettered:

> *Will you marry me? say you love me? call me tomorrow?*

Only one such mark punctuates a numbered or lettered series:

> *Will you tell me if (1) you love me, (2) you'll marry me, (3) you remember my name?* **No extra spacing.**

(2) Punctuate a parenthetical question (inside parentheses):

> *Sue Jones said (Can you believe it?) that she bought another horse!*

(3) Terminate a statement used as a question: *He said __that__?*

(4) Show doubt, uncertainty, or approximation:

John Jones is the President (?) of the company.
Omar Khayyam was a Persian poet (?-?1123).
She lived from 1803? to 1926.

A Question Mark Is Not Used:

(1) At the end of a courteous request phrased as a question, especially when you expect no answer: *Will you please send me a million dollars.*

(2) After an indirect question: *He asked if he would be allowed to go.*

Position With Other Punctuation:

The question mark immediately follows the question, whether or not it ends the sentence. If the question appears in the middle of a sentence, it is not necessary to follow it with a capital letter, nor is it necessary to use any additional punctuation, except possibly a dash:

Can such a thing happen? she wondered.
The question is "Who did it?"—not "Who said it?"

Position With Quotation Marks:

(1) Inside quotation marks if it belongs to quoted matter: *I ask you, "Is that true?"*

(2) Outside quotation marks if it's not part of the quoted matter: *Who said, "Kay never lies"?*

COMMA

The comma is the most frequently used, and the most frequently overused, punctuation mark. I have seen commas in the
most absurd places in sentences. I think some people heard
that a comma is to be inserted where you stop for a pause, and
whenever they stop to think of the next word to use, they stick
in a comma. That is not the comma's purpose. A comma separates written thoughts, not mental thoughts. Overpunctuating
usually complicates passages and increases keystrokes.
Furthermore, the exact meaning of a sentence can hinge on the
inclusion or omission of a single comma:

> *They didn't get married, because they wanted to live*
> *in peace. (They <u>didn't</u> get married.)*

> *They didn't get married because they wanted to live*
> *in peace. (They <u>did</u> get married, but not because*
> *they wanted to live in peace.)*

> *Jeff, my husband, is a neat guy. (Jeff <u>is</u> my*
> *husband.)*

> *Jeff, my husband is a neat guy. (Jeff is <u>not</u> my*
> *husband.)*

> *Please call Julie Barbara's secretary. (Secretary*
> *unnamed.)*

> *Please call Julie, Barbara's secretary. (Secretary*
> *named Julie.)*

A Comma:

(1) Introduces a direct quotation; terminates a direct quotation that is not a question, an exclamation, or at the end of a sentence; and encloses segments of a split quotation except when parentheses are used:

> *Mary said, "I heard him say, 'I love you (does he?) too,' but I don't believe him."*

(2) Separates elements in a series joined at the end by a coordinating conjunction like *and:*

> *We need a government of the people, by the people, and for the people.*

> *If it rains, if it pours, or if it sleets, the mail will be late.*

Some writers say you don't need this last comma, but I prefer to use it in all series. You'll never be wrong. Without the comma, there could be misunderstanding:

> *The application asked for name, address, sex and housing requirements.* (Sex requirements?)

The comma after the last element could also just replace the conjunction:

> *Michael Moneybags had a sister, a brother, a banker, a fortune teller.*

(3) Sets off conjunctive adverbs of more than two syllables, mild expletives, and interjections that are not essential parts of the sentence: *consequently, furthermore, darn, yes, no, well, however:*

> *This is, however, no laughing matter.*

(4) Sets off nonrestrictive elements:

> (a) *Because clauses.* In most instances, clauses beginning with *because* or *as* are nonrestrictive and should be preceded with a comma: *I love you, because you're a special person.*
>
> However, be careful that your sentence says what it's really supposed to say. In the first example on Page 9.12, *"They didn't get married because they wanted to live in peace,"* the comma makes all the difference.
>
> In the example, *"He did not go to the movie because he hated popcorn,"* did he not go for that reason? If not, what <u>was</u> the reason? A comma would indicate that a second, closely related thought is being introduced, and the fact that he did not go stands alone.
>
> (b) **For** *clauses.* The conjunction *for* (meaning *because*) is also usually preceded by a comma: *We hurried,* **for** *the car was leaving.*
>
> (c) **But** *clauses.* Even though it may seem nonrestrictive, a short qualifier phrase beginning with *but* does not need to be set off by commas: *He was from a distant* **but** *friendly city.*

(5) Separates <u>very short clauses</u> not joined by conjunctions:

I came, I saw, I left.
She knew, she was there, she saw it.

The commas take the place of the conjunctions.

(6) Sets off dependent phrases or clauses that precede the main clause. The ideas represented by those introductory words are usually *when, where, why,* and *how.*

Having made that decision, he turned to other matters." The main clause is "*he turned to other matters,*" but "*having made that decision*" introduces **why** he turned to other matters.

In another example, *"On Monday, she left early,"* the phrase "*On Monday*" tells **when** she left.

As an example of the necessity of commas in introductory phrases, consider: *To Mary Jane Kelly was someone special.* Without the comma, we don't know who is special to whom.

Note, however, that if the phrase or noun clause is the subject of the sentence, there is no comma: *Whatever is worth doing is worth doing well.* "*Whatever is worth doing*" is not an introductory clause—it's a noun clause and the subject of the sentence.

(7) Sets off interrupting transitional words and expressions like *on the contrary, on the other hand, I think.* These are fluff (see Chapter 7) and should be set apart: *The dog, I think, is still outside.*

(8) Sets off contrasting and opposing expressions:

> *He seems to have changed only his style, not his*
> *manners.*
> *The city is near, but not on, the coast.*
> *A holiday, but not a vacation day, is still available.*

Note that when *and/or, either/or,* or *neither/nor* join
items in a pair or series, the series is internally
unpunctuated:

> *I want neither the chocolate cake nor*
> *the ice cream for dessert.*

(9) Separates coordinate adjectives and phrases modifying the
same word and used where pauses should be, or *and* could be:

> *It was a bright (and) beautiful (and) sunny day.*

There should be at least three words in a series and they must
refer to the same word. Note that there is one comma fewer
than the number of words in the series. When the adjectives
are part of the concept of the noun, no comma is necessary:

> *She was wearing a bright red dress yesterday.*

It's the "red" that's "bright," and the two characteristics together
are part of the adjective modifying "dress."

(10) Sets off nonessential and parenthetic elements such as dependent clauses, participial clauses, and appositives—if they are not required to give a sentence or phrase meaning.

These nonrestrictive elements must be set off at the beginning and the end, unless the interruption is very slight. See the difference between *Tony, my brother, hit a home run,* and *Tony, my brother hit a home run.*

Most **of** *phrases* should be set off by commas because they are nonrestrictive modifiers. There is no comma in some nonrestrictive elements, however, because the appositive is so closely fused that it constitutes an essential element: *Lawrence of Arabia.*

But in the phrase, "*Kay duPont, of Atlanta, said. . .,*" the commas are necessary. When I become as famous as Lawrence of Arabia, I won't need the commas either.

Be careful not to use commas when a choice is being indicated, rather than an appositive:

> *Miss Smith, or Ann, will be honored* (Miss Smith's name is Ann).
> *Miss Smith or Ann will be honored* (one or the other).

(11) Separates independent clauses joined by coordinating conjunctions (*and, but, for, nor, or, yet, as, while*). **The comma alone cannot separate independent clauses, however; a conjunction is necessary as well.** Failure to use both will result in a run-on sentence unless the two main clauses are tightly connected and the actions occur at the same time: *We have tested the food and we are pleased.*

(12) Sets off words in
      direct address:

Let's shoot Millie!

Let's shoot, Billy.

(13) Indicates omission of a word, especially if the word (or words) has already been used in the sentence: *Vanilla ice cream is preferred by some people, chocolate, by others.*

(14) Sets off abbreviations in context if the abbreviation is preceded by a comma:

Letters, packages, etc., should go here.
Harry Smith, PhD, presided.
I work for Johnson Company, Inc., in the bank building.

(15) Sets off dates from a running text: *On December 17, 1941, Pearl Harbor was attacked.* Omit the comma between the month and the year if no day is specified, unless it's needed to punctuate construction of the sentence:

The notice I received in March 1990 was the first.
In December 1990, I finally paid it.

(16) Sets off expressions that introduce an illustration or example (*namely, for example*).

(17) Groups numerals into units of three (***100,000,000***). Generally not used with numbers in set combinations (***year 1991, Page 1411, 1127 Smith Street, Room 1112***).

Commas Should Not Be Used:

(1) To separate the subject from the verb or the verb from the complement:

> *A barefoot, tattered boy[,]leads two pets.*
> *January 1[,]is the first day of the year.*
> *I was told[,]I was getting a raise.*

(2) To separate modifiers from what is being modified:
White, ragged, fluffy[,] clouds.

(3) To separate two independent clauses without a conjunction: ***It was raining[,] he could not walk to work.*** Use a period or a semicolon.

(4) Between two parts of a compound predicate when their meanings are closely related and done at the same time:

He practiced the piano every day[,] and played very well.

Before she left for Hawaii, she did all the filing[,] and finished her other work.

(5) To set off restrictive modifiers: *The car[,] that I bought is a lemon. That* is restrictive, *which* is nonrestrictive. (See That/ Which, Chapter 8.)

(6) Between items in a series if they are simple constructions and joined by conjunctions: *I don't care whether it's chocolate[,] or vanilla[,] or strawberry.*

All of the rules for the comma can be summarized in two principles:

(1)   One comma separates two complete things; two commas set off some part of the sentence that needs to be distinguished from the rest of the sentence (fluff).

(2) If in doubt, don't.

Position With Quotation Marks: Always inside quotation marks, regardless of position in sentence or sentence structure.

COLON

The Colon Is Used To:

(1) Introduce something—usually a list, enumeration, or explanation: ***The following students were elected: Fays, Owens, Collins.*** Use two spaces between colon and explanation. Implies the phrases *as follows* and *the following* so you'll never need to repeat them:

> ***Here are the items on my order: china, crystal, silverware, a housekeeper, a house.***

> ***The members are: Marshall Mincemeat, Sergeant Searcher, Lieutenant Lionel, General Jerky.***

(2) Introduce lengthy quoted matter with or without a quotation mark:

> ***That young lady reminds me of an Oscar Wilde line: "We are all in the gutter, but some of us are looking at the stars."***

To introduce a short direct quotation, you may use a comma. Do not use a colon to introduce an indirect question or quotation.

(3) Follow the salutation in a typed business letter.

(4) Separate chapter and verse numbers (*Genesis 3:2*), volume and page numbers (*Volume 2:6*), and bibliographic references (*New York: Smith Publishing*).

(5) Divide numerals designating hours and minutes: *4:10 PM.*

(6) Introduce a clause or phrase (may be an independent clause) that explains, illustrates, amplifies, or restates what has gone before: *The sentence was poorly constructed: it lacked both unity and coherence.*

(7) Call attention to an appositive: *He had only one pleasure: eating.*

(8) Separate titles and subtitles: *CBS: Reflections.*

A colon has more effect than a comma, less power to separate than a semicolon, and more formality than a dash. It usually follows an independent clause and should not separate a verb from its complement: *He acted [:] quickly and wisely*; or a preposition from its object: *He went to [:] the movie.*

The first word after a colon should be capitalized when it begins a complete sentence.

Position With Quotation Marks: Always outside the quotation marks, unless quoting printed matter that contains a colon.

DASH

Two typed hyphens make a dash. A dash is a mark of separation more emphatic than a comma, less formal than a colon, and more relaxed than parentheses. It is **usually out of place in business letters** and should be avoided if possible.

The Dash Has Seven Unique Uses:

(1) To set off an abrupt break, interruption, or nonrestrictive element in a sentence—in other words, to show that some further explanation is coming: *My first thought on getting out of bed—if I had any thought at all—was to get back in again.*

(2) To suggest the pause that precedes a summary word or phrase: *They sold their house, their car, their children—everything they had.*

(3) To announce a long appositive or summary that contains commas: *The typewriter began to make a noise—a grinding, chattering, gritting rasp.*

(4) To show special emphasis, especially when a more common mark of punctuation seems inadequate: *Violence—the kind you see on television—is not helping our society.*

(5) Often to precede the attribution of a quotation: *"I never met a chocolate mousse I didn't like." —Kay duPont*

(6) To avoid confusion with parenthetical material or apposi- tives that are internally punctuated: *Three books—a dictionary, a thesaurus, and a novel—lay on the table.*

(7) To indicate hesitancy or indecision in dialogue (usually im- portant only to the fiction writer): *He said, "Well—I—uh— don't really—know."*

Position With Other Punctuation:

Any punctuation used with the dash is always placed next to the material to which it applies:

(1) Inside the dash if the punctuation applies to material inside the dash: *The faces of the victims—how sad!—were shown on TV.*

(2) Outside the dash if the punctuation applies to material be- fore the opening (or single) dash or after the closing dash: *Answer your question?—what was it?*

A dash is never used to end a sentence. When material intro- duced by a dash ends a sentence, use punctuation that is appropriate to the sentence as a whole: *I really do want to say—uh—well—you know—.*

A dash is never used beside a comma, colon, or semicolon. A dash may replace these marks for the purpose of avoiding confusion, for emphasis, or for joining: *I had to leave early—I just couldn't concentrate.*

Just remember that a dash should never be considered as a _substitute_ for a comma, semicolon, or period.

Position With Quotation Marks:

(1) Inside quotation marks if it belongs to quoted matter.

(2) Outside quotation marks if it's not part of the quoted matter.

ELLIPSIS

An ellipsis (three periods with spaces between) is used to show **omission, hesitation,** or **conformity.**

An Ellipsis:

(1) Indicates the omission of one or more words within a quoted passage, or a lapse of time, or a pause. If the omission occurs at the end of the sentence, you'll need four spaced periods (the last one represents the sentence stop).

(2) Indicates halting speech or an unfinished sentence in dialogue: *"I'd like to. . .that is. . .if you don't mind. . . ."*

(3) Is used as a leader (the horizontal guiding line between a chapter title and the page number it starts on). The line must be typed so that the periods are aligned vertically from leader to leader. Leave one blank space after the first chapter title before you begin typing its leader; then leave either one or two spaces after each subsequent chapter title for alignment. The leader itself is usually not spaced. Finally, leaders should end with one or two blank spaces before each page number. If leaders are separated by spaces, leave two spaces at each end; if not, leave one.

Position With Other Punctuation: The ellipsis is never used with punctuation marks other than an ending period.

Position With Quotation Marks: Always inside quotation marks.

Are you a Leader?

PARENTHESES

In Addition To Setting Off Parenthetical Material, Parentheses Are Also Used To:

(1) Set off directions, references, dates, and numbers or letters enumerating items in a series:

> *Statistics reveal (see Table 2). . . .*
> *A recent article (Hamption, 1981). . . .*
> *Three items are mentioned: (1) bread, (2) butter,*
> *(3) cookies.*

(2) Enclose arabic numerals confirming a typed-out number in legal correspondence: ***Please send two (2) bunnies to Mr. Peter Rabbit.***

(3) Indicate alternate terms and omissions: ***Please sign the enclosed form(s). On (date) we mailed. . . .***

Position With Other Punctuation:

A sentence containing an expression in parentheses is punctuated outside the parentheses exactly as if the parenthetical expression were absent. The expression within the marks is punctuated as if it stood by itself, except that the **final stop is omitted unless it is a question mark or exclamation point:**

> *I went to his house yesterday (it was my third attempt to see him!) but he had left again. He says, however (and why should I doubt him?), that he is not avoiding me.*

A period is not used inside parenthetical material, except with abbreviations:

> *She said, "Je t'aime" ("I love you").*
> *The conference was held at ABC (part of Alphabet Inc.).*

When a wholly-detached or independent expression or sentence is parenthesized, the final stop comes before the last parenthesis: *I am going. (You should too.)* This is the only time parenthetic material will begin with a capital letter, unless it is normally capitalized.

If a comma is needed after the phrase preceding the parenthetic insert, place the comma outside the closing parenthesis:

> *If you see Mindy (and surely you will), ask her to come see me.*

If a parenthetic insert falls at the end of a sentence, it's regarded as part of the whole sentence and the punctuation is placed outside the final parenthesis:

> *Was the report issued that long ago (1978)?*
> *We want to hear from you (the sooner the better)!*

When a parenthetic remark is part of a sentence but requires a question mark or exclamation mark of its own, punctuate the remark independently of punctuation required for the sentence:

> *They flatly refuse to explain their actions (frustrating, isn't it?).*

Position With Other Punctuation:

(1) Semicolon, colon, and dash are placed outside the parenthesis.

(2) No punctuation should be placed before the parenthetic material.

Position With Quotation Marks:

(1) Inside quotation marks if it belongs to quoted matter.

(2) Outside quotation marks if it's not part of the quoted matter.

(3) When quoted material is interrupted by parenthetic material that is unquoted, the quotation marks should be broken and renewed before and after the parentheses (or brackets): *Nancy said, "I will move to Rome" (Georgia, not Italy) "at the end of the year."*

BRACKETS

It's often thought that the main difference between parentheses and brackets is that parentheses are curved and brackets are angular. But there's more to it than that.

Brackets Are Used To:

(1) Set off extraneous data, such as editorial comments by someone other than the original speaker or writer: *He wrote, "I received your letter today [March 1]."* This insertion may clarify, comment, or identify a missing or incorrect letter or word.

(2) Function as parentheses within parentheses: *Henderson Act (22 Stat., Ch. 4, Sec. [or Title] 45, P. 50). (See Jones [formerly Smith and Jones] Company).*

(3) Enclose *sic,* which is used to tell the reader that the preceding misspelling, error, or incorrect usage is quoted exactly as it appears in the original.

Position With Other Punctuation: Same as parentheses.

APOSTROPHE

An apostrophe, despite its big name, is a little mark that has only two functions: It indicates **possession** and **omission.**

Possession (See also "Possessives," Chapter 8)

(1) Probably the biggest problem with apostrophes to indicate possession is when to use the extra _s_ when a word ends in _s_ or _z_. The experts still disagree, and almost all words in this category take _'s_. The use of _'s_ with words ending in _s_ or _z_ sounds formally depends on the pronounceability of the final syllable. If the syllable is pronounced, the _'s_ is usually used; if the syllable is silent, the apostrophe is retained but an _s_ is usually not added.

Kay's rule: If it has an _s_, don't add one; if it doesn't have an _s_, do add one. The apostrophe is mandatory and always follows the <u>base</u> <u>word</u>. *Charles', Keats', Gomez's, Knox's, class' , soldiers', boys', Jesus', Degas', Does', Moses', Joneses'.*

Pronouns are exceptions to the rule for possessives: *his, her, hers, its, their, theirs, our, ours, your, yours, my, mine.*

(2) Another common problem with indication of possession is where to put the _'s_ in joint possession, like *Mary and Jane's car.* This construction indicates <u>one</u> <u>car</u> owned by <u>two</u> <u>people</u>. If Mary owns a car and Jane owns a car (two cars), both names should get _'s_: *Mary's and Jane's cars.*

9.30

(3) When the plural form of the noun is irregular and doesn't end in *s*, like *men*, the possessive is formed by *'s*, just like singular possessives.

(4) The apostrophe is also traditionally used with expressions of time, measurement, and money, like *a week's pay, an hour's time.*

(5) An apostrophe is used to indicate understood possession: *The book can be found at your bookseller's.* You could easily add the word *store* to see the complete sentence.

(6) In a compound possessive construction, the apostrophe is attached to the last word: *I asked for Senator Jones of Florida's advice.*

(7) An apostrophe is used with *'s* before an action word (gerund):

I objected to the editor's changing my material.
I like the Beatles' singing.
I'm comfortable with his attending the meeting.

(8) The apostrophe is not used to show possession with modifiers ending in *s*: *a United States citizen, a General Mills product, an earnings statement, a sales quota.*

9.31

Omission

The apostrophe indicates omission of letters in word combinations (*isn't, you're, aren't, o'clock*). The apostrophe goes at the exact point where the letters or numbers are omitted except in irregular contractions like *won't (will not).*

The apostrophe is used in numerals indicating single years (*the class of '67*). An apostrophe is not used before or after a decade (*the 70s*).

Plurality

Apostrophes are never used to form plurals except for letters, figures, or words **when they are referred to as such:**

> *His 1's and 7's look alike.*
> *She has trouble pronouncing her the's.*
> *Mind your p's and q's.*

(Note that these elements are also underlined.) If it's the meaning or sense of the word rather than the word itself that's meant, no apostrophe is used.

Plural abbreviations do not have apostrophes (*1920s, GIs, CPAs, IRAs, MDs*). Plural names do not have apostrophes (*Joneses, Smiths, duPonts*) unless they are possessive (*the Smiths, but the Smiths' car*).

Position With Quotation Marks: Always inside quotation marks.

ASTERISK

An asterisk indicates a footnote. It is placed <u>after</u> the special word: ***The pamphlet called "Government Guide"* is helpful.***

Position With Other Punctuation:

An asterisk is placed inside a dash, and inside a closing parenthesis or bracket if it applies to the interrupting material.

Otherwise, the asterisk is placed outside all marks of punctuation, including quotation marks.

HYPHEN

This is the mark that some experts call the missing link, and Winston Churchill called a blemish to be avoided whenever possible. Basically, the function of a hyphen is to put two parts of a word under a single roof, and that is just about what the word denoted in its original meaning. It comes from the Greek *hypo*, meaning *under*, and *hen*, meaning *one*. See Page 6.6 for a list of hyphenated words.

The Hyphen Is Used:

(1) To mark syllable division at the end of a line, although this should be avoided whenever possible.

    (a) Always place the hyphen at the end of the first line, never at the beginning of the next line.

    (b) Divide only words of two or more syllables.

    (c) Divide only at syllable breaks.

(d) Never allow a single letter to stand alone.

(e) Never break a hyphenated word at the end of a line except at its normal hyphen.

(2) Between some prefix and root combinations (with no dividing space).

(a) In today's usage, a hyphen is not used after prefixes ending with vowels except when its omission creates a word that might be mistaken (a homograph). Several words beginning with *re* might be misunderstood: ***reform/re-form, react/re-act, recover/ re-cover, resign/re-sign.***

There are three exceptions to this rule: The prefixes ***ex, self,*** and ***all*** still take hyphens.

(b) Use between all prefixes and capitalized words: ***un-American.***

(c) Use between all prefixes and figures: ***pre-1990.***

(3) Between elements of a compound adjective or adverb when it precedes the modified word:

I found an old, half-eaten candy bar in my desk drawer.
He is a small-business man (as opposed to a small businessman).

There is a simple rule to use to decide which elements to hyphenate in a modifying phrase. If you have two or more modifiers preceding a noun, check each of them against the noun to see if it can stand alone with the noun.

For instance, *She is a good-looking woman.* Check to see whether *good* and *looking* apply separately to *woman.* Is she *good*? Is she *looking*? If neither, or only one of them, is applicable, the modifier must be hyphenated—*good-looking woman.*

Or: *Jack is building a two-car garage.* It may be a *car* garage, but is it a *two* garage? *Two-car* must be hyphenated. The same applies to three or more modifiers: *This is a run-of-the-mill example.*

Usually, however, a hyphen is not needed when the compound modifier is so well established that no ambiguity can result: *income tax laws, life insurance policies, public health program, real estate office.*

Attributive modifiers are not hyphenated when they end in *ly* or are as common as *very* and *most*.

(4) To suspend the first part of a hyphenated compound when joined with another hyphenated compound in attributive position: *Is this a six- or eight-cylinder computer?* Note the space.

(5) In phrases that express a single modifying idea: *Shirley, my mother-in-law, is a jack-of-all-trades.*

(6) Between the numerator and denominator in fractions used as modifiers. Fractions used as nouns are not hyphenated: *A two-thirds majority* BUT *two thirds of the people.*

(7) When the suffix *like* is added to a proper noun or a word ending in *l*: *cell-like, Kay-like.*

(8) With compounds composed of a number and a unit of measurement: *2-inch board.*

(9) With *well* and *ill* in attributive position, unless the expression carries another modifier: *a well-groomed woman* BUT *a very well groomed woman.*

(10) In numbers between *twenty-one* and *ninety-nine.*

(11) Between two different, yet equally important, functions: *secretary-treasurer.*

(12) To join a capital letter to a noun: *H-bomb, I-beam, U-boat.*

(13) To mean *up to and including* when used between numbers and dates: *Read Pages 1-7. I worked there June 1-15.*

(14) To compound two or more capitalized names (*New York-Chicago flight*), but not with a single capitalized name in attributive position (*New York flight*).

(15) When *elect* follows the noun, unless the office contains two or more words: *president-elect* **BUT** *vice president elect.*

(16) With compounds of a number and the suffix *odd*: *20-odd files*

Your common sense and a dictionary are your best guides. Just beware of your final syntax. A few years ago the *Chattanooga News* merged with *The Free Press*. Someone introduced a hyphen into the merger and obviously didn't pay attention to the syntax. The result was the *Chattanooga News-Free Press*. **When in doubt, leave it out.**

Positon With Quotation Marks: Always inside quotation marks.

QUOTATION MARKS

Single: Used primarily to enclose a quotation within a quotation: **Mary said, "I heard him say, 'I love you.'"**

Or a special word within a quotation: **Herman said, "That's 'bunk'!"** Italics may be used <u>instead</u> for this purpose.

Double: Used primarily to quote spoken material, which is always set off by a comma. Also used to:

(1) Set off titles of speeches, articles, captions, chapter and part headings, editorials, essays, headings, headlines, movies, plays, television and radio programs, papers, short poems, reports, songs, studies, subjects, and themes: **My novel, "The Revenant Curse," is a thriller.** Italics may be used <u>instead</u> of quotation marks.

(2) Indicate jargon, slang, or words being used in an unusual, contradictory, or arbitrary way:

> **Doesn't she look "great" today?**
> **You're a real "pumpkin."**

Italics may be used <u>instead</u> of quotation marks.

(3) Enclose words following such terms as *entitled, the word, the term, marked, designated, classified, named, endorsed, cited as, referred to as,* or *signed.* No comma between these words and the quoted material. Italics may be used <u>instead</u> of quotation marks.

Not used to enclose expressions following the terms *known as, called, so-called,* etc., unless such expressions are misnomers or slang.

(4)   Cite formal quotations as documentary evidence. No comma.

Not Used With:

(1)   Quotations of an entire line or more of either verse or prose if those lines begin on a new line and are indented, unless they appear in the original, as in dialogue. When the quote runs into more than one paragraph, use marks at the beginning of each paragraph, but at the end of the <u>last paragraph</u> only.

(2)   Proverbial expressions and familiar phrases of literary origin: *These are the times that try men's souls (and women's too)!*

(3)   Titles of works of art: paintings, statues, etc. (underlined or italicized).

(4)   Names of newspapers or magazines (underlined or italicized).

(5) Extracts that are indented or set in smaller type, or solid extracts in indented matter in text that already carries quotation marks.

(6) Indirect quotations.

(7) A display initial that begins a quoted paragraph.

Position With Other Punctuation:

(1) If the quote comes after the verb, a comma is placed in front of the first quote mark: **My mother said, "Don't worry about your heart until it's broken."**

If the quote comes before the opening phrase, a comma is placed inside the last quote mark: **"It is," I replied sadly.**

Single quotation marks always go inside double quotation marks, with no space separating them.

(2) The ending comma and period <u>always</u> go inside the quotation marks. This is always true even though they may seem not to belong there, like in a series: **We have the "touch," "feel," "difference," and "proof."**

(3) Colons and semicolons are always placed outside the quotation marks.

(4) Placement of question marks and exclamation points depends on the meaning:

> **The audience cried, "Bravo!"**
> **Please don't say "all is lost"!**
> **Why do you call some companies "outdated"?**
> **He asked, "Have you read 'The Time Is Now'?"**

(5) A dash is placed outside quotation marks unless the dash ends an uncompleted quote: **"I'd like to finish, but—" she said.** Note that there is no comma after the dash.

(6) When a parenthetic insert is a concluding part of quoted material, the final quotation mark is placed outside the final parenthesis: **"Yes," I said, "I love chocolate (not vanilla)."**

When quoted material is a concluding part of a parenthetic insert, the final quotation mark is placed inside the final parenthesis: **"Yes," I said, "I also love peanut butter." (Brenda said, "Me, too!")**

When an entire quotation is parenthetic, both sets of quotation marks are placed inside the parentheses: **I work too hard. ("Boil, boil, toil and trouble. . . .")**

When quoted material is interrupted by parenthetic material that is unquoted, the quotation marks should be broken and renewed before and after the parentheses: **She said, "My mind's made up" (as if she had one!) "to buy this car."** Note there are no separating commas.

(7) Do not double punctuation when quoted material is a concluding part of a sentence: **She asked, "When can I go
home?"**

There is one exception: When an abbreviated word ends
quoted material that also ends the sentence, the abbreviation
period is retained and the closing mark is used: **Were all the
boxes marked "K.D."?**

UNDERSCORE and ITALICS

Italics are now often used like underlining—to set off letters,
words, and phrases for special emphasis. Italics may also now
be used in place of underlining and quotation marks to set off
titles. So, if your typing machine has italics, use it instead.

If you're preparing copy for a printer, remember that the printer
will italicize any words you've underlined. If you actually
want words to be underlined, you need to indicate this in a
marginal note.

Use Underscore or Italics When:

(1) Emphasizing a word, phrase, or sentence that's important:

> **Wet paint. Do not touch!**
> **The first person in the office *must* make coffee.**

Keep in mind that this usage should be used sparingly. It's best
to get your point across with clear, concise writing so that
when you *do* use italics or underscore for emphasis, you'll get
the reader's attention quickly.

(2) Using foreign words likely to be unfamilar to the reader:

Charles has a *bon mot* for every situation.
This piece of music is meant to be played <u>andante</u>.
Joel was quite the *enfant terrible*.
I felt like I was experiencing <u>deja</u> <u>vu</u>.

You do not need to underscore or italicize foreign words that have been assimilated into English: **au gratin, en route, vice versa, status quo, per se, a la carte.**

(3) Referring to titles of works of art, movies, television/radio shows, paintings, books, magazines, newspapers, plays, long poems, and musical compositions. Other titles require quotation marks. Be careful to include articles (**a, an, the**)that begin titles; do not, however, italicize an article that is not part of the title: **the *Ladies' Home Journal*, *War and Peace*, *Newsweek*, *The New York Times*.**

(4) Referring to words as words, or letters as letters:

Remember to dot your <u>i's</u> and cross your <u>t's</u>.
There's a big difference between the words *affect* and *effect*.

(5) Citing the names of defendant and plaintiff in legal cases: <u>**Brown**</u> v <u>**The Board of Education**</u>. Note that *v* for *versus* is not underscored or italicized.

(6) Setting out headings and subheadings in reports and other documents (usually underscored, not italicized). Underscoring is not necessary if the heading is typed in all capitals.

(7) Formally defining words or terms, but only the first time: **The term <u>gross national product</u> means. . . .**

(8) Writing scientific names of plants and animals, **both genus and species.**

(9) Writing the names of ships, trains, aircraft, and spacecraft: **the *Queen Elizabeth 2*, the <u>Orient Express</u>, the *Enola Gay*, the <u>Enterprise</u>.**

Some General Guidelines:

(1) Use an unbroken line to underscore a phrase, heading, or sentence from beginning to end, not one word at a time.

(2) Do not underscore or italicize punctuation that comes directly after the underscored or italicized word or phrase in a sentence unless the punctuation is an integral part of the underscored material: **She has appeared in <u>Oklahoma!</u> and <u>Mame</u>.**

(3) When quoting, underscore or italicize any words that were emphasized in the original.

(4) When you emphasize words to call attention to key points, make sure all emphasized ideas are equally important and at the same level of abstraction. You'll confuse readers and distract from the main idea if you emphasize both a major point and a supporting point in the same section.

VIRGULE

A Virgule Is Used To:

(1) Separate alternatives: *and/or.*

(2) Separate successive divisions or months or years: *1990/91.*

(3) Represent *per* in numeral abbreviation combinations: *9 ft/sec, 90 m/hr.* Note the lack of periods.

(4) Represent division within an abbreviation: *B/L, L/C, C/D, B/D.*

(5) Serve as a dividing line between run-on lines of poetry in quotations: *I love you/Not for what you are/But for what I am/When I am with you.*

Think First!

CHAPTER 10: LETTERS

What's the best letter format to use?

FULL BLOCK

September 19, 19__

Reference: Request No. 2662

CERTIFIED MAIL
CONFIDENTIAL

Ms. Maryhad A. Littlelam
Fleece Animal Training School
Sheep Department
PO Box 123, Emu Station
Suretogo, GA 30067

Dear Ms. Littlelam:

SUBJECT: Block Letter

The most preferred business letter style today is the Full Block. It's the most efficient letter form, because it saves time and energy. It contributes to speed, simplicity, and ease—for the writer, typist, and reader. This is not to be used for personal letters.

In this style, everything, including the date and complimentary close, begins at the extreme left. This eliminates many mechanical operations in typing. As in all business letter styles, there is a double space between paragraphs.

This example shows the mixed punctuation form, which we use in the U. S. (colon after salutation, comma after complimentary close).

This is the style I recommend in all instances unless the dictator specifies a different style.

Sincerely,

M. Kay duPont, CPS
Vice President

bb

SIMPLIFIED

February 5, 19__

Mr. Littlejack Horner, President
Cherry Pie Unlimited
777 Corner Street
Plum, AR 72212

SIMPLIFIED LETTER STYLE

This style is gaining acceptance very quickly in the U.S. and Europe, Reader. It's already being used by many major organizations that want the speed of the Block style and believe the traditional salutation and complimentary close are outdated. It certainly cuts down on keystrokes, and it fits perfectly into a window envelope!

The only difference between Block and Simplified is the absence of the salutation and complimentary close, which eliminates the problem of choice.

The subject line is usually typed in all caps, flush left, not underlined. The signature line is also typed in all caps—**in this style only**.

Since no salutation is used, you should make it a point to mention the recipient's name in at least the opening and closing paragraphs of the letter.

This style has been sponsored by the Administrative Management Society since 1947, and is quite prevalent in the business world, Reader. I believe this is the letter style of the near future for all of us!

M. KAY DUPONT
VICE PRESIDENT

bb

Enclosure

c: Ms. Mary Contrary

MODIFIED

March 17, 19__
Request No. 2662

REGISTERED MAIL

Quick Candlestick Company
996 Burning Lane
Hotpants, AZ 85282

Attention Mr. Jack B. Nimble

Ladies and Gentlemen:

Subject: <u>Modified Letter</u>

This letter is an example of the Modified Block style letter. Modified Block differs from Full Block only in the placement of the date line, subject line, and signature block.

The date, reference, subject, and signature lines may be flush with the right margin (or as close as can be estimated), centered under the masthead, or aligned slightly to the right of center. Wherever you put them, the date, reference, and closing lines must be aligned with each other. As you can see, the inside address is blocked left and paragraphs are not indented.

Sincerely,

(Ms.) M. Kay duPont

bb

Encl.

cc: Mr. Jack B. Quick

SEMIBLOCK

October 31, 19__

HOLD FOR ARRIVAL

Mr. William Warlock
Vice President and Director
  of Bloody Marys
Witches' Brew Tavern
1313 Hobgoblin Trail
Halloween, Texas 66666

Dear Billy:

Subject: SEMIBLOCK LETTER

The Semiblock style is now considered old-fashioned and stiff, but some formal entities still prefer this style.

The first line of each paragraph is indented five spaces. The date is usually toward the right margin (can be centered), two to four spaces below the letterhead. All lines of the signature block are aligned with the first letter of the date. As you can see, the salutation line is not indented.

Have a happy holiday, Billy!

Cordially,

M. Kay duPont

bb

copy: Ms. Wanda Witch

Where do all the letter parts fit?

There are nine basic parts to an American business letter: Date, Reference Line, Mailing Instructions, On-Arrival Notations, Inside Address, Salutation, Subject Line, Body, and Signature Block.

DATE: Of course the first thing we need to do is put the date on the paper. The only hard-and-fast rule about that is to get enough sleep the night before to be able to remember it.

Placement of the date depends on the style of the letter. In a Full Block letter, you place the date at the left margin. In a Modified or Semiblock letter, it can be situated in the middle of the letterhead, toward the right margin, or slightly to the right of the center of the page. Always align the date with the signature block.

And always spell out the date on a business letter. On government letters, it's acceptable to put the day of the month first, without commas *(1 January 1990)*.

The date should be 2-6 (usually 4) lines below the masthead.

REFERENCE LINE: Include a reference line—with the file, correspondence, control, order, invoice, or policy number—when the addressee has specifically requested that correspondence on a subject contain a reference number. It's usually 1-4 lines (2 is common) below the date, wherever you put it, in full alignment.

10.5

SPECIAL MAILING INSTRUCTIONS: If a letter is to be sent any way other than regular mail (**certified, registered, special delivery, express,** etc.), indicate that on the letter. Align the mailing notation flush left in all letter styles, about four lines below the date (or two lines below the reference) and two lines above the inside address. Always type the mailing instructions in **all caps**.

ON-ARRIVAL NOTATION: On-arrival notations include *Personal, Confidential,* and *Hold for Arrival.* (Incidentally, *personal* means that only the addressee should open this letter; *confidential* means that the addressee's secretary or agent may open it.)

These **all-cap** words are blocked left in all letter styles, and positioned about four lines below the date and two lines above the inside address.

If you need both mailing instructions and an on-arrival notation, block the on-arrival notation directly beneath the mailing notation.

INSIDE ADDRESS: If you're writing specifically to an individual, the inside address typically includes:

    (1) Addressee's courtesy title and full name
    (2) Business title or department
    (3) Full name of the business
    (4) Company address

If you're writing to an organization, the address should include the full name of the company, individual department name (if required), and address. Of course you may include an attention line to a specific person in that department.

The inside address begins 3-8 (but never more than 12) lines below the date. It's always single-spaced and blocked left. For a professional look, try to **avoid abbreviations** in the inside address.

(1) Courtesy title: Always type a courtesy title before the addressee's full name if you're sure of gender. If you don't know the person's gender and can't figure it out, use no title at all in the inside address or the salutation.

None of us has any trouble with the courtesy title *Mr.*, but a problem sometimes arises when we are writing to a woman. Some women still sign their letters *Mrs. Jane Doe*, properly with the *Mrs.* in parentheses. If that's the case, you must address her as *Mrs.,* because that's what she prefers to be called. But when you don't know, as is more often the case, it is proper to just use *Ms.*

Then there's the courtesy title *Dr.* A doctor is a doctor whether she is an MD, a PhD, a DVM, or an honorary doctor. But if you address her as *Dr. Jane R. Smith*, do not use her academic degrees after her name. If you want to use her degrees, it's simply *Jane R. Smith, DDS*. This rule also applies to attorneys (*Nancy Bumperbut, Esq.* or *Billy Bumperbut, JD*).

The only title that comes after the name and also takes a courtesy title is one designating inheritance—*Jr., Sr., II, III,* etc. (*Mr. John R. Smith, Jr.*). Incidentally, the comma and period are now optional with a title designating inheritance (optional for <u>them</u>), and generation titles may be written in Roman numerals (*I, II*) or ordinals (*2nd, 3rd*). Follow your addressee's lead.

If your addressee happens to be plural, it becomes a little complicated:

Men: *Messeurs* or *Messrs.* duPont, Disend, Bradley, and Alexander
Messrs. Jim Smith and James Jones
Mr. James Jones and *Mr.* Jim Smith

Women:
Married: *Mesdames* or *Mmes.*, or separate names as above (with *Mrs.*)
Single: *Misses* or *Msses.*, or separate names as above (with *Miss*)
In general: *Mses.*, or separate names as above (with *Ms.*)

Male and female with different names (even if married): For two: Use two lines, with the man's name on the bottom line, or add *and* or a *virgule* and use one line:

Ms. Bertha Beautiful
Mr. Wallace Wonderful

Ms. Bertha Beautiful and Mr. Wallace Wonderful

Ms. Bertha Beautiful/Mr. Wallace Wonderful

Dr. Phyllis Physician and
Mr. Wallace Wonderful

For more than two: *Mr. T. T. Jones, Ms. L. C. White, Ms. M. K. duPont* or one line each

*See Page 10.14 for proper salutation forms.

10.8

Here's a list of other titles and how to write them:

Attorney:	Jane R. Blake, Esquire (or Esq. or JD) Ms. Jane R. Blake, Attorney at Law
State Attorney, Judge, Mayor, Governor, Cabinet Members, Congressperson, Senator, Representative:	The Honorable J. J. Jay
President:	The President
General:	General (or Gen.) George Patton, USAF (USMC, USN, etc.)
Ambassador:	The Honorable J. J. Jay American Ambassador Her Excellency Juanita Rodriguez Ambassador of Mexico
Chief Justice:	The Chief Justice of the United States
Consul, Consul General, Vice Consul:	Mr. Stick Billard, Esq. American Consul Paris, France The Honorable Chu Sumu China Consul Washington, DC
Professor:	Professor A. B. Galen, PhD Dr. A. B. Galen
Minister:	The Reverend Billy Graham The Reverend Dr. Graham

Priest:	The Reverend Thomas Graham
	The Reverend Dr. Graham
	The Reverend Father Thomas Graham
	The Reverend Father Graham
Rabbi:	Rabbi Jacob Stein
Cardinal in the U.S.:	His Eminence Thomas Graham
	His Eminence Cardinal Graham
Mother Superior:	The Reverend Mother Superior
	Reverend Mother Mary Jane Smith
	Mother Mary Jane Smith, Superior
Sister:	Sister Mary Jane Smith, RSCJ
	Sister Mary Jane Smith, SC

(2) Name: People value their names, so watch the spelling. If you were soliciting my business or my attendance at your function, and you misspelled my name after having seen it, I would not be as likely to accommodate you.

Of course there are times when you can't be certain about the spelling. If you don't have a definite spelling on a letterhead, call and ask. It may not be feasible to make a long distance call, but you can always make a local call. If you can't find out for certain, be very careful in your guessing.

Never address a letter to a woman using her husband's first name. Her first name is hers. Also, if she uses her maiden name, you should use it even if you know her married name, and it's especially important to use *Ms.* in this case.

If you're writing to a particular person in a company but you don't know their name and are forced to address the letter to, for instance, *Personnel Manager*, that title takes the place of a name. Of course if it's a local company, you can telephone to find out who the person really is. It doesn't take but a minute or two of your time to call, and it will impress people much more if they get a letter addressed strictly to them.

(3) Business Title: A business title, like *Secretary of State*, or *Purchasing Director*, goes underneath the person's name, **unless it is very short**, like *Director* or *President*, in which case it goes **after the person's name** on the same line. It may also be placed **before the company name** on <u>that</u> line. In these instances, always separate the title from the name with a comma, and never abbreviate. (You may abbreviate if the title is very long and on a line by itself.) Where to type the title is strictly a matter of the most well-balanced arrangement. **If a person holds two offices, use the higher title.**

(4) Company name: Be careful to type the name of the company correctly and **use the entire name**. In *The Words Incorporated*, be sure to include and capitalize *The*, and spell out *Incorporated*. For *Words and Phrases*, check the letterhead or phone book to find out if they use an ampersand (**&**) or *and*. Spell out the words *Company, Incorporated, Corporation*, or *Limited* unless the company itself abbreviates. Many corporations are now omitting the comma before *Inc.* If they do, honor their styling.

(5) Department: Spell it out and position it below the company name. You don't need to list both a business title and a department.

(6) Address: The best place to get the correct mailing address is from the addressee's own correspondence.

If they have a post office box, use that instead of the street address. It will be delivered quicker and it's easier and faster to type. There's not much point in putting the street address <u>and</u> the box number on the letter. Of course you don't need to write out "*Post Office* Box" and "*PO*" doesn't need periods or spaces.

You will need the street address for mail that needs to be signed for or delivered, and when there is no box number.

Use numerals in the street address—except *One*, which should be spelled out. Write out streets named *First* through *Twelfth,* but use Arabic numbers for any street number after *Twelfth.* If a numbered street over *Twelfth* follows a house number with no words in between, insert a spaced hyphen between them *(13 - 13th Street).*

Spell out *Street* and other variations, such as *Parkway* or *Avenue*, in the inside address. You many always abbreviate *Boulevard.*

There is usually a comma between the street name and any directional signals. Always capitalize directional letters. Periods are optional, but there are no spaces between the letters. If the directional signal comes <u>before</u> the street, write it out (*East 57th Street*).

If the company has a suite number, put it on the same line as the street address, with either a comma or two spaces between. The word *Suite* is written out. If it's too long to go on the same line, place it by itself on the line <u>above</u>.

Below the street address comes the city and state. You may abbreviate the name of the state with the proper two-letter abbreviations (**no period**), but I think it looks nicer in the inside address to write it out (except *DC,* which is always abbreviated). If you do, be sure you have enough *s's* and *p's* in *Mississippi*, and remember to put an <u>*s*</u> on *Illinois*, and an <u>*h*</u> on *Pittsburgh*.

The ZIP code has become very important in addresses since our postal system has become computerized. Even if your letter says "*Hartford CN,*" it could end up in Hawaii if it has Hawaii's ZIP on it. Get a good ZIP code book (available from the post office) and take the time to use it.

(7) Attention Line: If you have addressed your letter strictly to the company, the salutation will come two lines beneath the city/state/ZIP. But if you want to write to the company and direct the letter to a particular person's or department's attention, you need an attention line. This comes two lines under the city/state/ZIP line.

Write out the word *Attention* and place it at the left margin. **It is not written in all caps nor underlined.** Placement of a colon after the word is now optional. If you do use a colon, space twice and put the person's or department's name. If you don't use a colon, use regular spacing.

10.13

SALUTATION: Place the salutation 2-4 lines beneath the city/state or attention line, flush with the left margin. The colon (never a comma) is required in American styling on a <u>typed</u> letter.

The only courtesy titles that are normally abbreviated in the salutation are *Dr., Mr., Messrs., Mrs., Mmes., Ms., Mses., Msses.* Write out the others in a salutation, even if you abbreviated in the inside address.

If you're writing to one of those imaginary people who run departments but don't have a name, it's usually best to say *Dear Personnel Manager* (or whatever). If you're writing to the company itself, it's usually *Ladies and Gentlemen* (unless, of course, you're writing to an organization that is strictly female or male). You may also say *Dear duPont and Disend.*

If you have used an attention line, the letter is formally addressed to the company, so the salutation is to the company: *Ladies and Gentlemen.*

If, for some reason, you wish to say more than just *Dear*, as in *"My dear Mr. Fudpucker," dear* is not capitalized.

The proper salutation for a letter not addressed to any particular person or company, such as a letter of recommendation, is *To Whom It May Concern.* Remember that, when this salutation is used, there is no complimentary close.

<u>Salutations</u>

Two men:	Gentlemen Dear Messrs. Jones and Smith Dear Mr. Smith and Mr. Jones
Two Women: **Married:**	Dear Mesdames (or Mmes.) Jones and Smith (or separate names with *Mrs.*)

Single:	Dear Misses (or Msses.) Jones and Smith (or separate names with *Miss*)
In general:	Dear Mses. Jones and Smith (or separate names with *Ms.*)
Man/Woman with different names:	Dear Ms. Beautiful and Mr. Wonderful
One holds title:	Dear Judge Smith and Mr. Jones Dear Dr. and Mrs. (or Mr.) Smith
Doctor:	Dear Doctor (or Dr.) Smith
Attorney:	Dear Ms. Blake ("Esq." is never used in a salutation)
Judge:	Dear Judge Jay
Chief Justice:	Dear Madam (or Mr.) Chief Justice
Mayor:	Dear Mayor Jay Dear Mr. Mayor
Governor:	Dear Governor Jay
Cabinet members:	Dear Mr. Secretary
Congressperson:	Dear Congressperson Smith Dear Ms. Smith
Senator:	Dear Senator Jay
President:	Dear Mr. President Dear President Bush
General:	Dear General (Gen.) Patton
Ambassador:	Dear Mr. (or Madam) Ambassador Dear Ambassador Luce

10.15

Consul, Consul General, Vice Consul:	Dear Ms. (or Mr.) Smith
Professors:	Dear Professor Lee Dear Professors Lee and Rand Dear Professors Galen
Clergy:	Dear Dr. Lake Dear Professor Tyler ("The Reverend" or "Reverend" are not used in business salutations)
Minister:	Dear Mr. (or Dr.) Graham
Priest:	Dear Father Graham
Rabbi:	Dear Rabbi Stein
Cardinal in the U.S.:	Your Eminence Dear Cardinal Sheenan
Mother Superior:	Dear Reverend Mother Dear Reverend Mother Mary Smith
Sister:	Dear Sister Dear Sister Mary Angelica

SUBJECT LINE: Placed approximately two lines <u>beneath</u> the salutation. It must be flush left in Block letters, but you can center it in both Modified and Semiblock. Write out the word *Subject* if you use it at all, and you may use it with or without a colon, all caps or mixed, underlined or not. If you use a colon, space twice. You may also use the word ***Reference*** (although it rightfully belongs under the date), but the abbreviations ***Re*** or ***In Re*** should be reserved for legal work.

The subject line is used to put the subject on record, if only for the sake of the file clerk. But look what it can avoid:

> Dear Mr. Firebug:
>
> Referring to your communication of September 21 concerning a request of the Smoth Asbestos Company Inc. to have tests made in this department on samples from asbestos purchased in your area, let me say that our homeowners branch will be very glad to cooperate in this matter.

Of this whole complicated sentence, only the last portion belongs in the text of the letter. The rest is just so much dead-wood, through which Mr. Firebug has to burn his way before he reaches the searing issue. Obviously the most efficient system is the subject line:

> Dear Mr. Firebug:
>
> SUBJECT: Testing your Asbestos
>
> Thanks for your recent letter. We will be very happy to help you.

Notice the verb beginning the subject line—if your message involves action, show action on your subject line.

If the subject is long or multifaceted, use two lines and begin the second line under the reference item, not under the word *Subject*. If you need to list two subjects, **skip a line** between the first and second.

10.17

You may underline the subject material but, if you do, don't underline the word *Subject*. Also, don't underline each line of the reference information—just the final line. Underlining is discretionary, as are line lengths.

BODY: Begin the body of the letter about two lines below the subject line. Single-space internally and double-space between paragraphs.

Your letter should look **centered** on the page. The width of the side margins should be equal to the depth of the bottom margin. For example, if you've left an inch of space on the sides of the page, leave at least an inch of space at the bottom. The spacing, of course, depends on your letterhead style and letter length.

An attractive letter will look like a picture, with even margins working as a frame for the typed picture that is balanced under the letterhead. You should be able to accomplish that by planning ahead.

If a letter must have a second sheet, try to begin the second page with a new paragraph. If this is not possible, carry at least three message lines over to the next page. The signature block should never stand alone on a continuation sheet.

10.18

There are two ways to style a continuation sheet:

Flush left, about six lines from the top, preferably beginning with the addressee's courtesy title and full name, followed on the next line with the date, then the reference number if you have one, and finally the page number. This style is usually used with short copy.

> *Mr. Marvin Muskrat*
> *January 1, 19___*
> *Re: XYZ-298*
> *Page 2*

Across the top of page, with the addressee's last name at the left margin, the page number (in numerals) centered and enclosed with spaced hyphens, and the date aligned with the right margin—all on the same line. Leave 4-6 lines between the heading and the body. This style is usually used with longer copy.

> *Mr. Smithfield*   *- 2 -*   *January 1, 19__*
>   *XYZ-298*

SIGNATURE BLOCK:

(1) The **complimentary close** is the first line of the signature block. Place it two lines below the last line of the body. Its horizontal placement depends on your letter styling. In a Block letter, the close is flush left. In the other two styles, the closing is aligned under the date, wherever you have placed it. It should never, however, overrun the right margin.

Only the first word of the complimentary close is capitalized. A comma follows the closing word.

The most generally used closings in modern business correspondence are *Sincerely* and *Cordially.* Most writers have dropped the *yours* from these closings because it has no real meaning. Such closings as *Regards* and *Cordially* should be saved for people with whom the writer is on a first-name basis.

At one time, expressions like *I remain* and *I am* were used before, not in place of, complimentary closings, but they are considered too formal and excessive today. *With best wishes*, however, is still an acceptable expression before the complimentary close, and the shorter *Best wishes* may replace the closing.

(2) Name: Place the signer's name four to six lines beneath the close, always aligned directly beneath the close. (If the name is long enough to overrun the right margin, you may center it beneath the complimentary close.) Capitalize only the first letter of each element of the writer's name, and only the first letter of each major element of the writer's business title and/or department name (which go directly under the signature) if they are included. You may omit the business title and department name if they appear on the letterhead. The signer's name may also be omitted if it's on the letterhead— unless it's illegible. **Never type the name of the company in the signature block when using letterhead.**

Include any **academic degrees or professional ratings** of the writer after the surname so the recipient will know how to reply correctly, unless these designations are already included on the printed letterhead. They are never included in the written signature.

Courtesy titles need not be included in the signature line, unless the writer's name could belong to either a male or a female, or if the writer specifically <u>wants</u> his or her courtesy title specified. When this is the case, place the courtesy title **before the typewritten name,** in parentheses if desired:
(Ms.) Kay duPont.

If you sign a letter for someone else, put your initials immediately below and to the right of the writer's surname, or centered under their full name. The words *Dictated but not read* are not necessary; your initials indicate that you've been instructed to sign the letter. If you're writing under your own name but want the recipient to know your title, indicate it as *Assistant to Mrs. Bucklestein*, using only your manager's courtesy title and surname.

If two people need to sign a letter, follow the same guidelines for signatures, and style the double block in one of two ways:

(a) If there is room on the page, you can space one signature on top of the other, with one complimentary close and no typed lines:

Sincerely,

Jeffrey E. Disend
President

M. Kay duPont
Vice President

(b) If there is not enough room, you can space the signatures side by side, still using only one complimentary close, but this time with signature lines:

Sincerely,

Jeffrey E. Disend
President

M. Kay duPont
Vice President

(3) Identification Initials: You may omit the writer's initials. Do include typist's initials, however, for record-keeping. Align initials flush left in all letter stylings. Just about any format is OK.

A letter dictated by one person to be signed by another person, and typed by yet a third person, is shown this way: *AWM:COC:ls* (dictator:signer:typist). Never include *Jr.* or *Sr.* in initials unless they work for the same company.

(4) Enclosure Notation: If you need an enclosure notation, place it at the left margin, 1-2 lines beneath the identification initials (or signature block if there are no initials). You may write out the word *Enclosure* or abbreviate it *Enc.* or *Encl.* If there is more than one, you may type *Enclosures (3), 3 enc.*, or any variation thereof. If the enclosures are of special importance, or not specifically mentioned in the letter, list each of them numerically:

Enclosures: **1. *1994 Annual Report (2 copies)***
2. *List of major accounts*
3. *Profit and Loss Statement (1994)*

An attachment is considered an enclosure for purposes of this line.

(5) Copy Notations: A copy notation, now referred to as a courtesy copy, is also placed at the left margin, two lines below the last notation. You may use *Copy, Copies to:, cc, cc:, C:, c,* or just about any other form.

List multiple recipients of copies **alphabetically,** even if you show only their initials. If you use only surnames, always use courtesy titles. If you show first names or initials along with the last names, you may omit courtesy titles.

If the writer does not want the addressee to know that copies are being sent to other individuals, the copies are called *blind copies.* Place the blind copy notation (*bc*) and the name of the recipient in the **upper left-hand corner** of all copies on which the notation is to appear, styled as above.

(6) Postscript: Although many writers use them for emphasis, postscripts are not recommended for business letters. If you do use a postscript, place it 2-4 lines beneath the last notation. If your letter is Block style, the postscript is also blocked; if your paragraphs are indented, the first line of the postscript is also indented. While it is not incorrect to begin a postscript with the initials *PS*, it is now recommended that these initials be omitted. **A postscript should always be initialed by the writer.**

FOLDING LETTERS: For standard #10 envelopes: Fold up bottom third of letter, fold top third of letter over bottom third to within approximately one-half inch of the first fold. Insert the second fold in envelope first.

How have the postal regulations changed?

The Postal Service now requests that you use rectangular envelopes no smaller than 3 1/2" x 5" and no larger than 6 1/8" x 11 1/2". Type all addresses in a blocked, single-spaced format within the center of the envelope, at least 1" from the left and right edges, and at least 5/8" up from the bottom. No print should appear to the right or below this area. Address your envelopes in all caps, with one space between each unit and **no punctuation** except for the hyphen between ZIP units in nine-digit numbers. The USPS would like us to limit our address blocks to six lines vertically and 22 spaces horizontally.

The address should be single-spaced and blocked in the middle of the envelope, with all the lines having a uniform left margin. The entire envelope to the sides of, and under, the address must be blank.

Here's how it looks:

Nonaddress Information:	MKD 32683
Name:	MS M KAY DUPONT
Title:	VP OF MKTG
Company Name:	DUPONT AND DISEND INC
Attention (if no Name):	ATTN MS DUPONT
Address:	PO BOX 1212 GRAMMAR ST
Delivery:	ATLANTA GA 30305-1234

The postal computer will first scan the last two lines on the envelope, so your last two lines must contain all of the mailing address. That means that information like suite number, apartment number, station name, etc., should be on the same line as, and <u>after</u>, the street address. If your address is too long for one line, put the extra information on the line <u>above</u> the mailing address.

Don't forget the ZIP. Nine-digit ZIP codes are now in use and the ZIP is even more important than it used to be. Instead of just narrowing down the destination of mail to a particular post office, the new numbers precisely pinpoint mail's destination— the odd or even side of a block, the exact location of a building, and the exact suite number in a building. If the new ZIP will cause your delivery line to overrun the address block, you may move it to a line after the city/state line, blocked in the same format.

Special mailing notations and **on-arrival notations** should be typed in all caps on the line above the addressee's name, in the same block format.

Use the approved two-letter abbreviations for states (See list on Page 10.29). Use approved city abbreviations for cities over 13 spaces. These can be found in the Abbreviation Section of the National Zip Code Directory.

When typing a **foreign address,** refer to the sender's own return address for proper format. The name of a foreign country should always be typed in <u>all</u> <u>caps</u> as the last line of the block.

If you don't use the standardized address format on your envelopes, the automatic scanning devices won't be able to read the address and your mail will have to be sorted by hand, which is a time-consuming and letter-delaying job.

Abbreviations for Street Designators
and Words Frequently Used in Place Names

Academy	ACAD	Cove	CV	Haven	HVN
Agency	AGNCY	Creek	CRK	Heights	HTS
Airport	ARPRT	Crescent	CRES	High	HI
Alley	ALY	Crossing	XING	Highlands	HGLDS
Annex	ANX	Dale	DL	Highway	HWY
Arcade	ARC	Dam	DM	Hill	HL
Arsenal	ARSL	Depot	DPO	Hills	HLS
Avenue	AVE	Divide	DIV	Hollow	HOLW
Bayou	BYU	Drive	DR	Hospital	HOSP
Beach	BCH	East	E	Hot	H
Bend	BND	Estates	EST	House	HSE
Big	BG	Expressway	EXPY	Inlet	INLT
Black	BLK	Extended	EXT	Institute	INST
Bluff	BLF	Extension	EXT	Island	IS
Bottom	BTM	Fall	FL	Islands	IS
Boulevard	BLVD	Falls	FLS	Isle	IS
Branch	BR	Farms	FRMS	Junction	JCT
Bridge	BRG	Ferry	FRY	Key	KY
Brook	BRK	Field	FLD	Knolls	KNLS
Burg	BG	Fields	FLDS	Lake	LK
Bypass	BYP	Flats	FLT	Lakes	LKS
Camp	CP	Ford	FRD	Landing	LNDG
Canyon	CYN	Forest	FRST	Lane	LN
Cape	CPE	Forge	FRG	Light	LGT
Causeway	CSWY	Fork	FRK	Little	LTL
Center	CTR	Forks	FRKS	Loaf	LF
Central	CTL	Fort	FT	Locks	LCKS
Church	CHR	Fountain	FTN	Lodge	LDG
Churches	CHRS	Freeway	FWY	Lower	LWR
Circle	CIR	Furnace	FURN	Manor	MNR
City	CY	Gardens	GDNS	Meadows	MDWS
Clear	CLR	Gateway	GTWY	Meeting	MTG
Cliffs	CLFS	Glen	GLN	Memorial	MEM
Club	CLB	Grand	GRND	Middle	MDL
College	CLG	Great	GR	Mile	MLE
Corner	COR	Green	GRN	Mill	ML
Corners	CORS	Ground	GRD	Mills	MLS
Court	CT	Grove	GRV	Mines	MNS
Courts	CTS	Harbor	HBR	Mission	MSN

Mound	MND	Rock	RK	Switch	SWCH
Mount	MT	Rural	R	Tannery	TNRY
Mountain	MTN	Saint	ST	Tavern	TVRN
National	NAT	Sainte	ST	Terminal	TERM
Neck	NCK	San	SN	Terrace	TER
New	NW	Santa	SN	Ton	TN
North	N	Santo	SN	Tower	TWR
Orchard	ORCH	School	SCH	Town	TWN
Palms	PLMS	Seminary	SMNRY	Trail	TRL
Park	PK	Shoal	SHL	Trailer	TRLR
Parkway	PKY	Shoals	SHLS	Tunnel	TUNL
Pillar	PLR	Shode	SHD	Turnpike	TPKE
Pines	PNES	Shore	SHR	Union	UN
Place	PL	Shores	SHRS	University	UNIV
Plain	PLN	Siding	SDG	Upper	UPR
Plains	PLNS	South	S	Valley	VLY
Plaza	PLZ	Space Flight		Viaduct	VIA
Point	PT	Center	SFC	View	VW
Port	PRT	Spring	SPG	Village	VLG
Prairie	PR	Springs	SPGS	Ville	VL
Ranch	RNCH	Square	SQ	Vista	VIS
Ranches	RNCHS	State	ST	Water	WTR
Rapids	RPDS	Station	STA	Wells	WLS
Resort	RESRT	Stream	STRM	West	W
Rest	RST	Street	ST	White	WHT
Ridge	RDG	Sulphur	SLPHR	Works	WKS
River	RIV	Summit	SMT	Yards	YDS
Road	RD				

10.27

State Abbreviations

Alabama	AL	Montana	MT
Alaska	AK	Nebraska	NE
Arizona	AZ	Nevada	NV
Arkansas	AR	New Hampshire	NH
California	CA	New Jersey	NJ
Colorado	CO	New Mexico	NM
Connecticut	CT	New York	NY
Delaware	DE	North Carolina	NC
District of		North Dakota	ND
Columbia	DC	Ohio	OH
Florida	FL	Oklahoma	OK
Georgia	GA	Oregon	OR
Hawaii	HI	Pennsylvania	PA
Idaho	ID	Puerto Rico	PR
Illinois	IL	Rhode Island	RI
Indiana	ID	South Carolina	SC
Iowa	IA	South Dakota	SD
Kansas	KS	Tennessee	TN
Kentucky	KY	Texas	TX
Louisiana	LA	Utah	UT
Maine	ME	Vermont	VT
Maryland	MD	Virginia	VA
Massachusetts	MA	Virgin Islands	VI
Michigan	MI	Washington	WA
Minnesota	MN	West Virginia	WV
Mississippi	MS	Wisconsin	WI
Missouri	MO	Wyoming	WY

10.28

A Bibliography Of Useful Books On Writing And Style

Always get the latest versions possible.

Bates, Jefferson D. *Writing With Precision*. Washington: Acropolis Books Ltd.

Harper Dictionary of Contemporary Usage. New York: Harper & Row.

Holcombe, Marya W. and Judith K. Stein. *Writing for Decision Makers: Memos and Reports with a Competitive Edge*. Belmont, Cal.: Lifetime Learning Publications.

Kolb, Harold H., Jr. *A Writer's Guide: The Essential Points*. New York: Harcourt Brace Janovich.

Lederer, Richard. *Anguished English*. New York: Pocket Books.

Lederer, Richard. *Crazy English*. New York: Pocket Books.

Martin, Phyllis. *Word Watcher's Handbook*. New York: St. Martin's Press.

Meyer, Harold E. *Lifetime Encyclopedia of Letters*. Englewood Cliffs, N.J.: Prentice-Hall, Inc.

Miller, Casey and Kate Swift, *The Handbook of Nonsexist Writing*. Philadelphia: Barnes & Noble.

Strunk, William Jr. and E. B. White. *The Elements of Style*. New York: The MacMillan Company.

Style Manual. Washington: U. S. Government Printing Office.

Webster's Instant Word Guide. Springfield: Merriam-Webster Inc.

Webster's New World Dictionary, Third College Edition.
New York: Prentice-Hall, Inc.

Webster's Guide to Business Correspondence, Merriam-Webster Inc.

Webster's Secretarial Handbook, Second Edition.
Springfield: G. & C. Merriam Company.

Write Better, Speak Better Pleasantville, NY: The
Reader's Digest Association, Inc.

INDEX